D1446682

MARTHA STEWART

MARTHA STEWART

A Biography

Joann F. Price

GREENWOOD BIOGRAPHIES

GREENWOOD PRESS
WESTPORT, CONNECTICUT • LONDON

Library of Congress Cataloging-in-Publication Data

Price, Joann F.
  Martha Stewart : a biography / Joann F. Price.
    p. cm. — (Greenwood biographies, ISSN: 1540–4900)
  Includes bibliographical references and index.
  ISBN-13: 978–0–313–33893–9 (alk. paper)
  ISBN-10: 0–313–33893–0 (alk. paper)
 1. Stewart, Martha. 2. Home economists—United States—Biography.
3. Businesswomen—United States—Biography. I. Title.
  TX140.S74P75   2007
  640.92—dc22
  [B]   2007009603

British Library Cataloguing in Publication Data is available.

Library of Congress Catalog Card Number: 2007009603
ISBN-13: 978–0–313–33893–9
ISBN-10: 0–313–33893–0
ISSN: 1540–4900

First published in 2007

Greenwood Press, 88 Post Road West, Westport, CT 06881
An imprint of Greenwood Publishing Group, Inc.
www.greenwood.com

Printed in the United States of America

The paper used in this book complies with the
Permanent Paper Standard issued by the National
Information Standards Organization (Z39.48–1984).

10 9 8 7 6 5 4 3 2 1

To Bob, your love is a blessing; being with you is my salvation.
To Mom and Dad, how I wish you were here.

CONTENTS

Photo essay to follow page 53.

SERIES FOREWORD

In response to high school and public library needs, Greenwood developed this distinguished series of full-length biographies specifically for student use. Prepared by field experts and professionals, these engaging biographies are tailored for high school students who need challenging yet accessible biographies. Ideal for secondary school assignments, the length, format, and subject areas are designed to meet educators' requirements and students' interests.

Greenwood offers an extensive selection of biographies spanning all curriculum-related subject areas including social studies, the sciences, literature and the arts, history and politics, as well as popular culture, covering public figures and famous personalities from all time periods and backgrounds, both historic and contemporary, who have made an impact on American and/or world culture. Greenwood biographies were chosen based on comprehensive feedback from librarians and educators. Consideration was given to both curriculum relevance and inherent interest. The result is an intriguing mix of the well known and the unexpected, the saints and sinners from long-ago history and contemporary pop culture. Readers will find a wide array of subject choices from fascinating crime figures like Al Capone to inspiring pioneers like Margaret Mead, from the greatest minds of our time like Stephen Hawking to the most amazing success stories of our day like J. K. Rowling.

While the emphasis is on fact, not glorification, the books are meant to be fun to read. Each volume provides in-depth information about the subject's life from birth through childhood, the teen years, and adulthood.

A thorough account relates family background and education, traces personal and professional influences, and explores struggles, accomplishments, and contributions. A timeline highlights the most significant life events against a historical perspective. Bibliographies supplement the reference value of each volume.

INTRODUCTION

To her fans, Martha Stewart is a lifestyle empress, a diva of domesticity, and the do-it-yourself doyenne. They also believe she is a misunderstood visionary. To her detractors, she's taken the American woman backwards, espousing an unobtainable ideal. She's known as a living brand and is deemed a cultural icon. Her meteoric rise to popularity and to cult status hardly seems possible. She's parodied and jeered and some say she's forcing today's woman into a homemaking fantasy. Martha Stewart is loved, hated, emulated, and envied; she's also one of the most successful businesswomen in history. According to Sarah A. Leavitt, author of *From Catharine Beecher to Martha Stewart*, "Altogether, she is perhaps the most famous female brand name in the American consumer world, and she continues to expand her holdings and projects."[1]

Martha Stewart's homemaking career began when she opened a catering business that she operated out of her home. The business flourished and her reputation quickly grew. With the success of her home-based business, she launched her career as a domestic advisor with the publication of her first and highly successful book, *Entertaining*, published in 1982.

Although domestic advice providers have been around for many years, Martha Stewart has made it a profitable industry. One example of her popularity could be seen at the 1996 Rhode Island Flower and Garden Show, held in Providence. Martha was the featured speaker at the luncheon and her topic was gardening and her own garden at Turkey Hill, her home in Westport, Connecticut. A month before the event, the Providence newspaper asked readers to write about their devotion to all things "Martha." The newspaper received dozens of responses. The resulting story, written by Keren Mahoney Jones, was titled "Mad about Martha: Stewart's Rhode Island Fans Try to Live Her Way."

One woman wrote that she hand made dolls, bottled her own vinegar, and dried flowers; another wrote that she made Christmas ornaments out of old chandeliers. Another woman wrote: "I find the magazine (*Martha Stewart Living*) both informative and useful. Many of the ideas in the magazine are practical and useful for everyday living, but some are just plain fun to look at—read—and maybe even daydream about a little."[2] Still another devotee noted that "we usually dine on Corningware rather than Lenox, but oh! The fantasies are wonderful."[3] These women, like so many others, profess their love and admiration of all things "Martha," even though many certainly identify what she espouses as domestic fantasy.

There are, of course, women who scoff at Martha and what she teaches. One woman wrote in her letter to the newspaper: "One year I watched Martha Stewart on TV making her own wrapping paper from old, brown paper bags and gold spray paint. Poor Martha, what a mess! She went to so much trouble, too—cutting the bags, spraying curlicue designs, waiting for the paint to dry. It took quite a long time and then when she wrapped her gifts, they looked so homely! I could have told her that a jumbo roll of wrap was on sale at Ocean State Job Lot for only $1.00, but who was I to spoil her Christmas?"[4] This letter also expresses what many women feel is Martha's obsession with do-it-yourself homemaking.

Author Sarah Leavitt, a self-proclaimed Martha admirer, wrote: "The Rhode Island women and others who share their devotion to Stewart know that she is a businesswoman. They understand that she has a staff of professional designers and gardeners to help her and that the ideas she brings forth usually need to be adapted according to budget and lifestyle. They harbor no illusions that their homes could conform to her television-set image of the perfect house. But they appreciate her ideas. They want to make their lives, or at least their daydreams, more delicious, more unique, more decadent, more inviting."[5]

On the day of the luncheon, when author Sarah Leavitt asked Martha if she thought her work as a domestic advisor had a historical precedent, Martha responded that she had gotten many story ideas from nineteenth-century advisors and keeps many of their works in her office. Leavitt notes that domestic advisors have always been aware of social issues and have helped educate women. They know that writing about the home has been important to American culture for more than a century. Domestic advisors, Martha included, are social commentators and domestic education for women has remained a vital part of American life.

Martha Stewart is also known as a trendsetter and, most certainly, a cultural icon. In his book *How Brands Become Icons*, Douglas B. Holt defines cultural icons as symbols that people accept to represent important ideas and that people or things are widely regarded as compelling symbols of ideas or values that society deems important. He adds: "From Nelson Mandela to Ronald Reagan. . .from Oprah Winfrey to Martha Stewart. . .cultural icons dominate our world. . .icons serve as society's foundational compass points, anchors of meaning continually referenced in entertainment, journalism, politics, and advertising."[6] To many, Martha Stewart fits this definition. Rising from a modest upbringing in a working-class neighborhood in New Jersey, she has been for many years, a powerful force and a trendsetter in business, fashion, and certainly in the media.

Martha Stewart is seemingly everywhere, seen by some to completely saturate American media. She appears daily on television and radio and her successful magazine *Martha Stewart Living* is on the newsstand. Her other magazines, *Everyday Food* and *Blueprint*, are also on the newsstand and doing well in ad revenue and subscriptions. Martha is regularly in the newspaper and often appears at events around the country. Her line of home wares at Kmart brings her products to one audience and her extravagant wedding and entertaining ideas to another. Her Web site provides information through bulletin boards, live chats, and a direct link to her catalog. Shortly after her release from prison, she announced she would be designing homes with homebuilder KB Homes, yet another high visibility relationship for Martha and her beloved corporation Martha Stewart Living Omnimedia.

Martha's life is discussed, her statements cursed, and what she will do next is always anticipated. For years, she's been the subject of late night comedy skits and is often a parodied by those who don't understand her, are jealous of her, wish they could be just like her, or are sure they aren't like her at all. In our fame-crazed culture, she's known as a lifestyle trendsetter, a media magnate, and as ubiquitous as the Internet. She's also a convicted felon, and is described as indomitable and a survivor. To some she is an inspiration, and to others, she's the epitome of shallowness and a model to be avoided. To everyone, at the very least, she's interesting, and always attention-grabbing. From her marriage in 1961, to the birth of her daughter, Alexis, in 1965, to a brief career as a securities trader, to her move to the suburbs in Westport, Connecticut in the early 1970s, to a best selling author in the 1980s, and to one of the most powerful and successful businesswomen in the 1990s, to her incarceration at Alderson Prison, through the ups and downs, the successes and failures, the life of the ubiquitous Martha Stewart is always a fascination, a fairy tale story that continues on, always captivating millions around the world.

Her life is a story that is both a how-to and a how-not-to live. It is the story of a woman with an attitude that says perfection is attainable, a perfection that both drives her and creates the problems that have always plagued her and contributes to the glee that many feel at her downfall and to her staying power.

Martha has survived a difficult divorce, raised a successful daughter, and took a home-based catering business to a successful multimillion dollar corporation. In early 2005, she was released from a minimum-security prison after serving time for lying to investigators about a stock sale. Never one to go any speed but full speed ahead or to let anything stand in her way, Martha used much of her time in prison to plot her return with careful precision. After her prison release and wearing her famous ankle bracelet worn while under house arrest, she developed and then starred in a new daytime television show and in her own version of *The Apprentice*. She also wrote another book, and although some suggested her business empire was crumbling and her reputation was in tatters, she moved on, always mindful of, but not influenced by, those who said it couldn't or shouldn't be done.

For Martha Stewart, it is always up to her, and whether you love her or hate her, there is always a buzz around her, no matter what she does or says. The question remains, will Martha Stewart, as a living brand, a cultural icon, be overexposed. Douglas B. Holt says in his book, "An icon must possess integrity, demonstrating its commitment to advancing the values espoused by its myth. When a brand appears to be taking advantage of its followers' allegiance to the myth for quick commercial gain, the brand hemorrhages credibility and loses its effectiveness."[7] Will there always be a Martha Stewart brand? Will there always be a "Martha phenomenon" or will women who idealize her come to believe her standards are too high, her level of domesticity too complicated, and her projects a fantasy in our fast paced world?

Three generations have now known Martha Stewart. They've read about and viewed her meteoric rise and downfall. Her life is like that of a modern Cinderella, only we don't know yet if she will always wear the latest, best-designed glass slipper. Martha Stewart's life is always filled with drama and controversy, leaving her fans and detractors to question, wonder, clap, and dream. She makes her own rules and always goes at a speed few can match. Standing in her way isn't at all wise. After all, in America, everyone loves a comeback, no matter how many there are.

NOTES

1. Sarah A. Leavitt, *From Catharine Beecher to Martha Stewart: A Cultural History of Domestic Advice* (Chapel Hill: University of North Carolina Press, 2002), 199.

2. Ibid., 2.

3. Ibid.

4. Ibid., 201.

5. Ibid., 2–3.

6. Douglas B. Holt, *How Brands Become Icons* (Boston: Harvard Business School Press, 2004), 1.

7. Ibid., 189.

TIMELINE: EVENTS IN THE LIFE OF MARTHA STEWART

1905	Martha Stewart's paternal grandfather, Franz Josef Kostyra, born in Poland in 1879, arrives in New York.
August 21, 1911	Edward Kostyra, Martha Stewart's father is born.
April 17, 1911	A record 12,000 European immigrants arrive at Ellis Island.[1]
1920	Frank and Helen Kostyra move to Jersey City, New Jersey. The Prohibition Amendment takes effect; "speakeasies" open as taverns and saloons close.[2]
1929	Edward Kostyra graduates from Dickinson High School. October 29 The stock market crashes and by November 13, unemployment reaches 3.1 million.[3]
1933	The Unemployment Relief Act is passed. Unemployment reaches 1 million, five times the unemployment rate of 1931. Prohibition, which began 13 years before, ends and is widely celebrated.[4]
1937	Edward Kostyra meets Martha Ruszkowski, Martha Stewart's parents. After a short courtship, the two are married.
1938	February 8: Andy Stewart, Martha's future husband, is born to George and Ethel Stewart. May 13: Eric Kostyra is born, Edward and Martha's first child and Martha Stewart's brother.

1941   August 3: Martha Kostyra Stewart is born, Edward and
        Martha's second child and first daughter.
        December 7: Japan attacks the United States at Pearl Harbor;
        Japan also attacks Manila, Singapore, and Hong Kong. The
        United States declares war on Japan. The United States soon
        enters the war in Europe after Germany declares war.

1942   Single men between the ages of 18 and 35, and married men
        between the ages of 18 and 26, are eligible for the military
        draft.

1944   The Kostyra family moves from Jersey City, New Jersey, to
        Nutley, New Jersey.

1945   May: Germany surrenders and the war ends in Europe.
        August: Japan surrenders and the war ends in the Pacific.

1955   Andy Stewart graduates from Putney High School in Ver-
        mont. He enrolls in the University of Virginia in the fall.

1956   A total of 77 percent of college-educated women marry;
        41 percent work part time, 17 percent full time.[5]

1958   College tuition doubles since 1940 and is expected to double
        again by 1970; the average cost is $1,300 a year.[6]

1959   Martha Kostyra Stewart graduates from Nutley High School.
        She enrolls in the Barnard College for Women in the fall.

1960   Spring: Martha meets Andy's sister, Diane Stewart Love.
        Martha then meets Andy for the first time.
        Summer: Martha and Andy begin dating and later in the year,
        Andy meets the Kostyra family for the first time.

1961   February: Andy proposes marriage to Martha.
        March: Andy and Martha are engaged.
        July: Andy and Martha are married.
        August: Martha appears in the popular back-to-school edition
        of *Glamour* magazine as one of the ten best-dressed college
        girls in 1961.
        Julia Child publishes her famous cookbook *Mastering the Art
        of French Cooking*.

1962   Andy graduates from Yale Law School. He enrolls in a gradu-
        ate program at Columbia University.

1963   President John F. Kennedy is assassinated in Dallas, Texas.
        Vice President Johnson is sworn in as President.
        Julia Child first appears on television and the art of cook-
        ing French food through demonstrations begins and soon
        becomes very popular.

1964   January: Andy finishes his graduate degree studies.

June: Martha graduates from Barnard College with a degree in art history.

1965   Early in the year, Martha discovers she is pregnant.
       September 27: Alexis Gilbert Stewart is born.
       Martha and Andy purchase a home in Middlefield, Massachusetts; they undertake a remodeling project that takes them nearly five years to complete.
       December: Martha hosts her biggest party yet, a Christmas party for friends and colleagues to celebrate the holiday and to introduce their baby daughter.
       President Johnson pledges his support for South Vietnam. The first U.S. combat troops land in the country; 25,000 march in Washington, D.C. to protest the war.

1968   August: Martha passes the securities examination and is hired by New York brokerage firm Monness, Williams & Sidel.

1971   Martha and Andy purchase a home in Westport, Connecticut, which they name Turkey Hill Farm.
       Gourmet magazine circulation doubles since 1967 to 550,000 and gourmet food industry rapidly expands.[7]

1973   Martha resigns from Monness, Williams & Sidel.
       Martha and Norma Collier form a 50/50 partnership and open The Uncatered Affair.
       Andy leaves Bangor Punta Corp. as their corporate lawyer, and joins Abrams Publishing, a book imprint of the Times Mirror Company.
       It is estimated that one out of three meals is consumed out of the house, compared to one in eight in 1965.[8]

1975   Martha and Norma dissolve their partnership. Martha opens The Market Basket at the Common Market in Westport, Connecticut.

1977   January: Martha incorporates as Martha Stewart Inc.
       Spring: Andy is diagnosed with cancer.

1979   August 31: Edward Kostyra, Martha's father dies.
       Health foods sales reach $1.6 billion ($140 million in 1970). The divorce rate increases 69 percent since 1968, with the median duration of marriage at 6.6 years. Approximately 40 percent of children born during the decade will spend some time in a single-parent household.[9]

1980   The economy suffers under a third year of double-digit inflation. The divorce rate grows from one in three marriages in 1970 to one in two marriages. The Sony Walkman, cordless telephones, and 24-hour-a-day news coverage (CNN) first appear.[10]

1982   Martha publishes her first book, *Entertaining*.

1983   June: Alexis Stewart graduates from Putney High School and enrolls in Barnard College in the fall.
       Martha publishes *Martha Stewart's Quick Cook*.

1984   Martha publishes *Martha Stewart's Hors d'Oeuvres*.

1985   Martha publishes *Martha Stewart's Pies and Tarts*.
       Sam Waksal establishes ImClone Systems.
       Salad bars, ethnic restaurants, wafer thin pizza, pastas with ingredients like goat cheese and broccoli, whole-grain pita bread, and ice-cream substitutes are all popular.[11]

1986   Martha's first TV show, *Holiday Entertaining with Martha Stewart* airs.
       Fitness foods that are high in fiber and low in sodium, fat, and cholesterol are popular.[12]
       An increased number of consumers seek professional assistance with home decorating.[13]

1987   Martha publishes *Weddings*.
       Martha signs a contract with Kmart to be their national spokeswoman and a consultant for home fashions.
       April: Andy moves out from Turkey Hill Farm.
       July: Martha purchases the historic Adams House in West-port, Connecticut. The refurbishment of the home is later featured in her book *Martha Stewart's New Old House*, pub-lished in 1992.
       A total of 60 percent of kitchens have microwave ovens; 40 percent of the food dollar is spent eating out.[14]

1988   March: Andy files for divorce.
       Martha publishes *Martha Stewart's Quick Cook Menus*.

1989   Nonfat frozen yogurt, upscale takeout food, and American bistros are very popular.[15]

1990   Summer: Martha and Andy's marriage ends as the courts issue a final divorce decree.
       Fall: Martha publishes *Martha Stewart's Gardening Month-by-Month*.
       November: *Martha Stewart Living Magazine* first appears on newsstands.
       Peter Bacanovic goes to work at ImClone Systems.

1991   June: Martha signs a 10-year contract with Time Warner Inc. to publish *Martha Stewart Living Magazine*. The contract provides for TV programs, videos, and books. Martha begins appearing on the NBC *Today* show.

1992   Martha publishes *Martha Stewart's New Old House*.
Peter Bacanovic leaves ImClone Systems and becomes a stockbroker at Merrill Lynch.

1994   Martha publishes *Martha Stewart Menus for Entertaining* and *Holidays*.
Oprah Winfrey's personal chef publishes a best-selling cookbook.[16]

1995   Martha negotiates a new contract with Time Warner Inc.
Martha publishes *Handmade Christmas*, *The Martha Stewart Cookbook*, and *Special Occasions*.

1996   Martha publishes *How to Decorate: the Best of Martha Stewart Living*, *What to Have for Dinner*, *Great American Wreaths*, and *Martha Stewart's Healthy Quick Cook*.
Oprah Winfrey's talk show is the highest rated talk show in TV history since its syndication in 1986.[17]

1997   Martha purchases *Martha Stewart Living Magazine* from Time Warner, Inc., and gains complete control of editorial content.
Martha publishes *Christmas with Martha Stewart Living*.
Martha moves from the NBC *Today* show to CBS's *This Morning*.

1998   Martha publishes *Decorating Details* and *Desserts: Our Favorite Recipes for Every Season*.
Sales of rich foods and cookbooks like *Cooking with Two Fat Ladies* increase, as obesity rates increase; the nation is obsessed with health food and vitamin supplements.[18]

1999   Martha publishes *Arranging Flowers* and *Martha Stewart's Hors d'Oeuvres Handbook*.
October: *Martha Stewart Living Omnimedia Inc.* goes public on the New York Stock Exchange. Martha owns approximately 70 percent of the stock.

2000   Martha publishes *Gardening from Seed* and *Parties and Projects for the Holidays*.

2001   Martha publishes *Martha Stewart Living Annual Recipes* and *Good Things for Organizing*.
Martha surpasses Oprah Winfrey as the most written about woman in America.
December: Sam Waksal expects the FDA will approve the marketing of ImClone's anticancer drug Erbitux.

At Christmas, Sam, his stockbroker Peter Bacanovic, and Martha leave separately for holiday vacations. As Martha is on her way to Mexico, Peter Baconovic's assistant, Doug Faneuil, contacts her about ImClone stock.

December 28: The FDA notifies Sam of their decision not to allow ImClone to market Erbitux.

2002 Early in the year, investigators take an interest in ImClone Systems and possible insider trading activities.

Martha publishes *Martha Stewart Living Annual Recipes*.

September: Martha receives notice from the Securities & Exchange Commission that civil insider trading charges may be imminent.

September: Doug Faneuil, Peter Bacanovic's assistant at Merrill Lynch, pleads guilty to a misdemeanor in his part of insider trading charges.

October 15: Sam Waksal pleads guilty to fraud and perjury charges.

2003 Martha publishes *The Martha Stewart Living Christmas Cookbook*.

May: Martha introduces a new line of furniture design and moves forward to launch a new magazine called *Everyday Food*.

June 4: After refusing to accept any plea bargains, or agreeing to any settlements, Martha is indicted for obstruction of justice and securities fraud by the U.S. Attorneys Office in New York City. She steps down as Chairman and CEO of Martha Stewart Living Omnimedia and is given the title of Chief Creative Officer.

2004 January 27: Martha's trial begins.

February: Doug Faneuil testifies for three days.

February: Ann Armstrong, Martha's personal assistant, testifies.

February: Mariana Pasternak, Martha's longtime friend and traveling companion to Mexico in December 2001, testifies.

March 3: The jury receives the case.

March 5: Martha hears the guilty verdict.

July 17: Martha is sentenced to five months in jail and five months house arrest.

September 15: Martha holds a press conference where she announces she will begin serving her sentence, despite a pending appeal.

October 8: Martha enters Alderson Federal Prison for Women in Alderson, West Virginia.

December: It is announced that Martha will have a new daytime TV show to be called *Martha* and a prime-time show called *The Apprentice: Martha Stewart*, both to premier in the fall of 2005.

2005   March 4: Martha is released from Alderson Prison and flies home to Cantitoe Farm in Bedford, New York.

March: Martha addresses her staff at Martha Stewart Living Omnimedia to announce her new vision for the company.

April: *Time* magazine publishes its annual list of the world's most influential people that includes Martha on the list of builders and titans.

April: *Martha Stewart Living* magazine has the headline "Welcome home, Martha."

August: Martha's ankle bracelet is removed and her house arrest ends.

October: Martha publishes *The Martha Rules: 10 Essentials for Achieving Success* and *Martha Stewart's Baking Handbook*.

Martha announces a 24-hour program on Sirius Satellite Radio to be called *Martha Stewart Living Radio*.

2006   August 7: Martha reaches an agreement with the SEC to settle her insider trading accusations.

NOTES

1. Lois Gordon and Alan Gordon, *American Chronicle* (New Haven: Yale University Press, 1999), 109.

2. Ibid., 202.

3. Ibid., 283.

4. Ibid., 323.

5. Ibid., 538.

6. Ibid., 556.

7. Ibid., 681.

8. Ibid., 699.

9. Ibid., 753.

10. Ibid., 766.

11. Ibid., 811.

12. Ibid., 820.

13. Ibid., 811.

14. Ibid., 829.

15. Ibid., 847.

16. Ibid., 896.

17. Ibid., 906.

18. Ibid., 932.

Chapter 1

WHAT IT MEANS
TO BE MARTHA

―――――――――――――――

There are many, many people who have inspired, taught,
influenced, and supported me during the years that I have been
visualizing, creating, building, and managing my own
entrepreneurial venture. I want to thank every one of them
for their efforts, energy, help, and advice. The construction of
Martha Stewart Living Omnimedia has been a meaningful and
exciting journey—not just for me, but also for each and every
colleague who has spent time with me, designing and erecting and
maintaining a fine, worthwhile, productive American dream.
　　　　　　　　　—Martha Stewart, *The Martha Rules*

Martha Stewart is a workaholic who thrives on pressure. Who and what
she is and all her successes cannot be denied. What she has accomplished
has been earned through hard work and a great deal of tenacity. Martha
knows only one way to live and one way to do business and that is living
life to the fullest and always moving full speed ahead.

Many identify with her and want to be just like her. Others are sure
they don't want to be like her at all. Taking risks is one trait that has followed this domestic diva from her childhood through today. Her career
of being "Martha" and all that this means began early under the tute-
lage of a two-parent household in a working-class neighborhood. From a
domineering, perfectionist father, Martha learned gardening and carpentry
skills and so much more; her mother guided her homemaking and sewing
skills. She later honed these skills and acquired many more on her own,

and she uses them everyday. When she and her former husband, Andy Stewart, renovated their first farmhouse not long after they were married, the experience became a springboard for Martha to do what she was good at and what she loved to do—renovation, design, project management, and domestic advice. All of these became important talents that she used extensively and expertly to further her ever evolving career.

Martha is said by some experts to be a societal phenomenon. She has integrated family, the home, and the workplace with unique and traditional gender roles in order to succeed. She identifies with her legions of readers and viewers by who she is, what she says, what she does, and perhaps most important, how she presents herself. They know she is serious in the advice she dispenses. They believe her when she lectures on making the perfect pie, sewing the most unique Halloween costume, or covering the prettiest lampshade. She has wide appeal to millions in America and around the world, and what she espouses in the home and even in the workplace offers challenges, rewards, pleasure, and achievement. She takes the mundane and makes it unique and even gives it the opportunity to be interesting and worthwhile.

In the meanwhile, she had effectively managed her fortunes; indeed she has amassed millions by engaging women, and many men too, into the pleasures and necessity of domestic work. She has the exceptional ability to teach what she knows and discuss what she advocates in a way that gives her fans what they need, want, and easily accept as significant to family, home, and traditional values. Her personal vision has made her one of the wealthiest women in America.

Martha reaches her community of followers through books, television, radio, Web sites, and her popular magazines. Although she is known as the queen of domesticity and a domestic diva, she never portrays herself as dowdy, or only belonging in the kitchen. Indeed her demeanor reflects a polished professional, and serious expert. She is ultimately a businesswoman who teaches others how they can be better than who they are, either in the kitchen, the boardrooms, or anywhere in between. Although she isn't a trained chef, or an electrician, or a horticulturist, she uses her versatility, skills, and sense of style to teach her viewers and readers how best to bake a chocolate cake, repair a lamp, or cultivate orchids. She is creative, intellectual, and self-determined. This is what it means to be "Martha."

Mentors often play an important role in the development and continued achievements of successful entrepreneurs. Martha's father was her first and perhaps most important mentor. As the oldest daughter in a family of six children, Edward Kostyra directed Martha's every move to a level of perfection that to many seems unattainable. Martha inherited that extreme level of perfection and the drive to always succeed from her father. This trait is still an important part of who Martha Stewart is today.

From a modeling career that began in high school and that didn't give her the success she craved, to a marriage that ended in divorce, to raising a successful daughter, to a highly successful career as a securities trader, to her career as a domestic advisor and lifestyle trendsetter that began when she opened her catering business out of her own home, Martha has defied societal pressures and male-dominated industries to succeed. With some luck, a lot of drive, and a great deal of self-determination, Martha never looks back. By the time she published her first book, *Entertaining*, in 1982, she knew she wanted to be more than a caterer. She set her sights higher, to be *the* expert, *the* domestic diva, and lifestyle empress to both the elite and the masses.

In her book *The Martha Rules*, Martha Stewart stated:

> I believe that each phase of my career has been intriguing to people in part because of what preceded it. My image developed as a person who was willing to take risks and try new things. There are so many people who dream about changing their lives; the media know the public loves to be informed about someone who has dared to go out and do it.[1]

It is true that this woman from humble beginnings in a working class neighborhood in New Jersey did make a life of great wealth, influence, notoriety, and expertise.

Martha is, and has been for many years, a cultural icon, a living brand, a do-it-yourself doyenne, and an often misunderstood visionary. She is also one of the wealthiest and most powerful women in America. Based on her own vision, her own perspective, and her own rules, and with an average of four hours of sleep each night, she is constantly on the move, always looking for new opportunities and ways to transform women's lives.

Martha may have set the bar too high for most women. She may offer only a homemaking fantasy that draws women in but does not allow them to achieve such a level of perfection. Martha Stewart is seemingly everywhere and often saturates American media. Nearly everyday, she is on television, on the radio, or on her Web site where you can download advice, recipes, shop for her branded items, be a part of a live chat, or see what she doing in the kitchen. You can thumb through the pages of her successful *Martha Stewart Living* magazine, *Everyday Food*, *Blueprint*, or *Body + Soul* magazine. You can visit a furniture store and see her line of furniture, shop at Kmart and see her line of home ware, paint your walls with her brand of paint, use branded photo products at Kodak, or look for a new home and see what Martha-branded residences look like. You can catch her at events across the country or see her interviewed on news programs.

Martha's life has been carefully watched, discussed, parodied; what she will do next is anticipated with gloom or glee. Some are jealous of her, some despise her, and some view her as a reminder of their own inadequacy. Others want to be just like her and try to imitate her. In our fantasy-crazed culture, she's a trendsetter and an icon. She might be modeled or avoided, but at the very least, she's always interesting, and only a few people in her self-imposed inner circle know what she will do next. Whether she is loved or hated, there will always be a buzz about her because that is what Martha wants. After all, she did go to jail on her own terms. She determined when she would serve the time and afterward, she made a successful comeback that she and her inner circle carefully orchestrated. The question is whether Martha Stewart, and what is known as "Martha" and all that means will, be overexposed.

Three generations have witnessed her rise, seen her fall, and then watch her rise again by sheer will and more than a bit of luck. Anyone can speculate on what she will do next, but only she knows for sure. Martha puts it this way:

> Perhaps the question I'm most asked is 'How do you do it all?' The answer is quite simple. I'm organized. Not fanatically organized like some of my friends, whose shelves of books are neater than those in the Library of Congress, nor like others whose clothes are categorized by color, season, size, and length. But organized enough so that I don't feel disorganized, or sloppy, or frantic, and, when pressed, I know I can put my hands on that photo, or memo, or book, or birth certificate that someone needs that day. My life is extremely busy. I have more than one home, and really more than one job.[2]

How could such an intelligent, experienced, proficient woman nearly destroy all that she worked so hard to accomplish? How could she risk everything over a stock trade that in the end meant so little to her financially and then serve time in a federal prison after refusing to make a deal or to admit that perhaps she was wrong?

In her book, *The Martha Rules*, she says:

> I had spent my career and built my company's reputation working hard to bring Good Things to as many people as

possible. And yet a personal stock trade was threatening to destroy everything: my successful television show, my much-loved magazine and book projects, a nationally syndicated radio show, a vibrant product design and merchandizing business, and a highly creative staff that was never at a loss for ideas. Wall Street valued us, our growth was good, and our prospects were extremely bright.[3]

Perhaps Martha herself was to blame for the legal problems that nearly destroyed her career. Or perhaps overzealous investigators wanted to make an example of a highly successful businessperson and a powerful, wealthy woman. After all, in so many instances, America holds powerful women to nearly impossible standards. Martha may have been a scapegoat, an example of what was wrong in corporate America.

The investigation, March 2004 conviction, incarceration, and home confinement were more than difficult for Martha, who had always lived life at a frenetic pace, making her own way and her own rules. But to everyone on the outside, at least, Martha persevered and never wavered. She always said she acted in good faith and denied the allegations against her. In her book, *The Martha Rules*, Martha said: "The last three years have been filled with so many unwanted distractions, but I have persevered, kept my optimistic outlook, and tried my best to keep in touch with all of my wonderful supporters."[4]

Alexis, very much her mother's daughter, who has her own entrepreneurial spirit and sense of independence, and who steadfastly stood by her mother's side, especially during the difficult trial and while Martha was in prison, said:

> Nothing my mother has shown the world can do any harm. Don't we all want a better life? No matter what they say about my mom, all she ever does is teach the world good things that will help them in life. So what if she shows you the perfect way to do it? She's not showing off. Would you want your professor at school to do anything less in any other subject? So what if she aspires to do everything perfectly? Don't we all try to do that? At least most of us do. Why tear her down for that? Go tear down the porn kings or the fast-food chains or other people who feed trash to your children. My mom has never spoken a bad word about anyone who has talked unkindly about her. I know that for sure.[5]

Martha Stewart is a true career woman. Her goals include glorifying the home and the family environment and to give her readers and viewers traditions to follow. She has always been serious about her focus to create an environment that is beautiful and inviting for everyone, using themes like comfort and ease. It is this dedication and commitment that makes her, and her alone, Martha Stewart. And for those that admire her, that is truly a "good thing."

What makes Martha who she is today, a diva, an icon, a teacher and a leader? It is more than her humble beginnings. It is more than her marriage and her daughter. It is more than family and friends, mentors and experiences. Without a doubt, it is more than a drive to succeed and a dedication to perfection. But put it all together, and this is Martha Stewart.

NOTES

1. Martha Stewart, *The Martha Rules* (New York: Martha Stewart Living Omnimedia, 2005), 101.

2. Martha Stewart. *Good Things for Organizing* (New York: Martha Stewart Living Omnimedia, 2001), 2.

3. Stewart, *The Martha Rules*, 153.

4. Ibid., 69.

5. Lloyd Allen, *Being Martha* (New Jersey: John Wiley & Sons, 2006), 219.

Chapter 2

GROWING UP IN NEW JERSEY

*A hyper-competent perfectionist who grew up with a sewing
needle in one hand and a hammer in the other.*
> —Laura, about her older sister

*My father was supercritical. And Martha is very demanding.
It's a family curse.*
> —Eric, about his younger sister

On a sunny August day in 1941, in the working-class community of
Jersey City, New Jersey, Martha Kostyra Stewart was born. At the time
of her birth, Franklin D. Roosevelt was President of the United States.
That fall, the New York Yankees defeated the Brooklyn Dodgers in the
World Series; and the film *Rebecca*, taken from the novel by Daphne du
Maurier, won the Oscar for best picture. In 1941, America was still reeling from the devastating effects of the Great Depression that began in the
1930s, and many Americans were still hoping that President Roosevelt
would keep the country out of the war that was raging in Europe. Even
though the United States was not yet sending soldiers to fight overseas,
gasoline was rationed in the eastern part of the country. When American soldiers joined the Allied forces in the war by the end of 1941, just
after the Japanese attack at Pearl Harbor on December 7, gasoline was
rationed throughout the country. As part of the mobilization for war, to
be fought on two fronts, in Europe and in Asia, the production of auto-
mobiles for private use was soon halted, and a short while later, important and widely used commodities such as sugar, coffee, and butter were

also rationed. Everyone was encouraged to have a garden, soon known as "Victory Gardens," to grow their own food. Patriotism in many forms flourished. Young Martha was Edward and Martha Ruszkowski Stewart's second child and their first daughter. Her older brother, Eric, was born in May 1938 and four more children would soon join the family.

What influenced Martha Kostyra Stewart and contributed to what she would eventually become included her Polish heritage, her grandparents and parents, life in America just after the Great Depression and the war years that followed, and her growing up in a small home, in a large family, in a working-class neighborhood in New Jersey. The oldest Kostyra daughter would eventually be known as one of the most powerful businesswomen in history and also one of the wealthiest women in America. She would also be known as a domestic diva, a cultural icon, a lifestyle guru, and a living brand.

MARTHA KOSTYRA STEWART'S FAMILY

Franz Josef Kostyra and Helen Krukar Kostyra: Martha Kostyra Stewart's Paternal Grandparents

Franz Joseph Kostyra came to America from Poland in 1905. At that time, many immigrants were sailing into New York harbor from Europe, some having no formal education, most hoping to begin a new life far away from the problems they faced in their homeland. Arriving in New York with no formal education, Franz Joseph had served in the military guard and as a cook in the army mess hall, skills he was determined to use in his new country. When he arrived in America, he changed his name to Frank and, using his cooking and mess hall management skills, he quickly found a job in a restaurant and soon became involved in managing the day-to-day operations that included hiring and training kitchen workers and developing recipes.

Remaining true to his Polish roots by living and socializing in the Polish community of New York City, Kostyra met Helen Krukar at a Polish social club. They soon married. Living close to Helen's family, Frank worked at a restaurant and Helen worked in the household of a wealthy New York family. In the summer of 1911, Helen gave birth to a son, Edward Kostyra, who would years later be Martha Kostyra Stewart's father.

In 1920, after working for the same restaurant for 15 years, Frank Kostyra moved his wife and son to Jersey City, New Jersey, believing this working-class community would provide more financial opportunities.

There he opened a butcher shop, using the money he had diligently saved over the years working in the restaurant. In 1925, he sold the business to his brother-in-law and began to buy and sell other businesses. He also was a moneylender, providing loans to individuals who might otherwise not be able to obtain credit. The Kostyras also purchased a local bar and renamed it Kostyra's Tavern. The family lived in an apartment on the second floor. By this time, Frank and Helen had two sons and a daughter; but it was the oldest son, Edward, who, from the time he was born and throughout his life, was the apple of his mother's eye.

Joe and Franciska Ruszkowski:
Martha Kostyra Stewart's Maternal Grandparents

Joe and Franciska Ruszkowski came to America from Poland before World War I. Living in Buffalo, New York, Joe Ruszkowski became an ironworker, a job he held for the rest of his life. The couple had four children. Their firstborn was a girl they named Martha, who later became Martha Kostyra Stewart's mother. Franciska worked as a seamstress to earn extra money for the family and taught her two daughters to sew. Martha Sr. became a dressmaker, a skill she later passed along to Martha and her other daughters. Believing that their children should all receive an education, Martha went to college to become a teacher. Her two brothers also benefited from higher education, one becoming a lawyer and the other an engineer.

Edward Kostyra and Martha Ruszkowski Kostyra:
Martha Kostyra Stewart's Parents

From the time he was born in 1911, Edward Kostyra was his mother's favorite, and throughout his life she spoiled him, believing he was a genius, someone everyone should marvel at, and someone who would be successful. Always knowing he was the apple of his mother's eye, Edward thought himself to be an expert on many things and believed he was special. Throughout his life, he convinced others that he was indeed intelligent and extraordinary.

Unlike other boys his age, Edward enjoyed cooking, sewing, and gardening and early on, had an interest in design and fashion. Many of his mother's friends envied her having a son with such unique and helpful interests and skills. Despite his unusual interests, however, he was not considered to be feminine. Taking after his father in size and looks, Edward was over six feet tall, with curly blond hair and blue eyes. Also like his father, he had an interest in horses and was always curious about how things worked or were designed. Edward could often repair things, using his quick and curious mind to take them apart and fix them again. He also had a talent for being able to look at something and then copy it, or study something and know all about it. Frank Kostyra, Martha Stewart's younger brother, once described his father as having unique mind power, saying he could walk into a kitchen, smell something cooking or baking, identify the ingredients, and bake or cook it himself. Frank Kostyra added that his older sister, Martha, had inherited this talent from their father and that such skills were in the blood, in their very genes.[1]

In 1929, Edward graduated from Dickinson High School with a general curriculum diploma. Having been advised by his high school gym teacher to study physical education, he enrolled at the Panzer College of Physical Education and Hygiene in Orange, New Jersey. While studying physical education, Edward took an interest in art. He also studied English, sociology, and psychology. Despite his college major, he wasn't thought of as an athlete and was more often described as a dreamer. Despite the ongoing Depression in America, young Edward decided that touring Europe was a necessary part of his education. His mother financed such a trip, which allowed him to further his studies abroad. When he returned home from a summer overseas, Edward had many stories to tell and photographs to show friends and family about his trip.

In the summer of 1937, Edward met Martha Ruszkowski at a seminar in Pennsylvania. By this time, Edward had worked for the Jersey City School District as a gym teacher, a job he was offered right after college graduation. Even though jobs were scarce during the Depression, he was able to obtain a position through his father's connections with members of the local city government. Believing that this teaching position did not match his talents, Edward enrolled in evening college classes to further his education, ultimately hoping to find a career that was both more satisfying and more lucrative.

Martha Ruszkowski had just graduated from college and had accepted a position in Slogan, New York, to teach elementary school at the beginning of the fall term. Before beginning this assignment, she became pregnant and the couple decided to marry. After an elopement, Martha Sr. fulfilled her one-year teaching contract, and then moved to Jersey City, New Jersey, where she and Edward rented a small apartment. According to Martha, in her book *Weddings*, her parents "fell madly in love, eloped, and then married formally in a church in December 1937." She also wrote that her mother looked "radiant, dressed stylishly in rust silk velvet with her gorgeous hair gathered into a golden bronze kerchief. In all her portraits, she smiles as beautifully as Leonardo's Mona Lisa."[2]

Their new life together, as a working-class family living a working-class life, was a disappointment to Edward, who still thought of himself as special and certainly destined for something better. In 1938, their first child, Eric, was born. In August 1941, Martha, named after her mother, joined the family. Four months later, America entered World War II. During the war, Edward worked on the docks at the shipyard in New Jersey. He never served in the military but instead served on the home front.

Financially, it was a difficult time for the Kostyras. With two small children, Edward's meager salary barely covered the rent on a tiny second-floor walkup where there was no porch and no room for a garden. Edward's mood greatly influenced the daily life for the Kostyras. He resented having to support his wife and children rather than live the kind of life for which he felt he was destined—a life filled with music and art, nice clothes, and good meals. In his book, *Martha Inc.*, author Christopher Byron describes their family life at the time: "The Kostyra family seems to have inhabited a rather joyless world revolving around Eddie, the father, in a seeming state of perpetual anger at his wife for placing the limitations of parenthood on his life. There was fighting, quarreling, and relentless bickering over money, of which there was apparently never enough."[3]

In 1944, with two children and a third on the way, the Kostyras moved from Jersey City to Nutley, New Jersey, a quiet working-class community just a short bus ride from New York City. The family moved into a small, three-bedroom, one bath, two-story home they purchased with a down payment provided by Edward's mother. In her book *Martha Stewart's New Old House*, Martha describes the home at 85 Elm Place, as "an ordinary frame house on a crowded street" and "modest but friendly, originally covered in a wide, crinkled asbestos-type siding. It was situated on a small lot and had a front yard with a sidewalk, a very narrow driveway wide enough for exactly one car, and a long, rather narrow backyard...the three bedrooms were really not large enough for our family of eight, but space never seemed to be a problem." She added that the house had a "full and really very good basement where we cooked, laundered, did small carpentry projects and worked on hobbies."[4]

With 2,000 square feet of living space and only one bath for what would eventually be a family of eight, the Elm Place home quickly became overcrowded. There always seemed to be someone in someone else's way and any discussion, whether it was a quiet one or something far louder, was easily heard by everyone.

By the end of World War II, with war-related work ending at the shipyard, and with three small children to support, Edward was unemployed. By the time Martha was five years old and ready to enter kindergarten, Edward found a new position as a pharmaceutical salesman. As a physical education major in college, he had enjoyed his classes in biology, chemistry, and health, and the position seemed like a good fit for this outgoing and charming man. His first sales position was with Pfizer, Inc., a company that provided a base salary and commissions. To young Martha, her father's new job meant a summer day at Coney Island, hosted by the company. To Edward, the new job meant a company-owned automobile. To the Kostyra children, the new car meant added chores.

In his book, *Being Martha*, Lloyd Allen notes that every Sunday, the Kostyra family would worship at the Polish Catholic Church. The girls were dressed in their pressed pinafores and the boys in their pressed shirts and ties. On the way home, the family would stop at the Polish bakery and then return home, where the children changed into their work clothes. With rags and a bucket full of soapy water, the children's Sunday task was to wash Edward's company car, a 1950 steel-gray Chevrolet Bel Air, which he liked to keep looking sharp. This chore, of all those assigned to the children, was perhaps the most difficult. Edward was known for his high standards and he wasn't an easy man to please. When the Kostyra children said they were finished, Eddie would inspect their work as the children held their breaths, their wet rags at their sides. Pointing to a lone smudge, he would say, "You missed a spot."[5]

Always trying to earn more money and recognition, both of which he felt he deserved, Edward often changed jobs, always trying to negotiate a better salary and more perks with another company. Sometimes Edward was unemployed, which meant Martha Sr. had to find work to help support the family. For a time, she returned to the classroom at a parochial school, where she could teach without a teaching certificate from the State of New Jersey.

In the Kostyra household, perfection and cleanliness were the norm and the expectation. George Stewart, Martha's youngest brother, recalled that his father was quite brutal in his demands; if anything was on the floor that wasn't supposed to be there, everyone knew to grab a broom and sweep it up. George noted that, to this day, both he and Martha have the cleanliness trait and that his sister is a clean freak and likes everything spotless. He noted that when they were growing up, their home was a place where you "didn't curse, kiss, and you washed your hands a lot."[6]

Edward Kostyra has been described as a self-absorbed narcissist who blamed the world for never allowing him to live up to his expectations.

He is also known as one of the most powerful forces in his oldest daughter's life. In his book *Martha Inc.*, Christopher Byron writes that Edward always set standards of excellence and intolerance that became dominant characteristics of Martha's own personality as well.[7]

As an adult, Martha often reflected about her family life and growing up in Nutley, New Jersey. In September 1996, Martha wrote in her "Remembering" column about how her father promised her mother he would modernize the kitchen, something she says he had promised to do since purchasing the home in 1944. "It took twelve years to save the money for a new floor and new cabinet . . . her father often had enough money for expensive clothes and for his own hobbies including amateur photography." She added that many of her father's projects didn't turn out very well.

In her "Remembering" columns in *Martha Stewart Living* magazine, Martha often wrote about her family life. For many Americans at the time, the topic of conversation was often advances in technology, including the new color television sets that were quickly replacing the black-and-white sets found in most American homes in the early 1950s. While many were in awe at the new invention, the Kostyras didn't have a black-and-white set until the end of the 1950s, the last family on their street to have one in their living room. In September 1997, she wrote that when her father finally bought a television set, he placed it in the living room so that he, sitting in his favorite chair, had the best view. The other members of the family, Martha noted, were forced to sit elsewhere, squinting and straining to see the screen.

Edward blamed himself for the family's lack of money and his personal circumstances, but he also blamed his family for putting him there in the first place. In a February 1997 "Remembering" column, however, Martha remembered her father as a man possessing creative talent, and someone who taught her gardening and decorating. She also noted that her father's demand for perfection was valuable in any activity, something he taught her, made sure she understood, and something that has been evident throughout her life. Writing about her father in her book, *Martha Stewart's Gardening*, Martha wrote, "Some of my most vivid memories of childhood come from those early March days when my father I would plant seeds indoors. Our preparation was meticulous." In the acknowledgments, she wrote, "Most of all, my thanks to my father, for being my first teacher of gardening. His love of growing things was transferred to me though [sic] our gardening together; I will remember what he taught me forever." She tells her readers that she remembers planting seeds indoors with her father and spending long hours with him during Christmas vacations carefully reading each catalog and deciding what to order.[8]

In the introduction to *Martha Stewart's Pies and Tarts*, Martha wrote about her father's love of the earth and how he was forced to cut down the family's old apple tree because its large shadow cast too much shade over his other beloved plants and flowers. She recalls studying gardening books with him: "Choosing what we would like to have on an imaginary estate, as well as what we could actually afford to have and take care of."[9]

By September 1953, the family home was crowded and Martha—a seventh grader at Nutley Junior High School—had little privacy, something most young women need at that age. Living in a house with only one bathroom, Martha complained that she never had any privacy. In the February and March 1993 issues of *Martha Stewart Living* magazine, she wrote in her "Remembering" column that she was still bothered by the fact that she was forced to wash her hair in the kitchen sink because the family used the one in the bathroom for brushing teeth.

As the oldest daughter, Martha helped raise her five brothers and sisters and also helped with the household chores throughout her teen years. She noted later that she was like a second mother to her siblings. She shared a bedroom with her sister Kathy, the fourth child of the Kostyra family. The bedroom was furnished with a double bed and a chest of drawers; closet space was divided between them. Martha's mother once said of her eldest daughter that she had the habit of taking the hem of her nightgown and using it to dust the top of her dresser. She tried to teach one of her friends to dust this way and when her friend did it at home, her mother yelled at her.[10]

Even with her responsibilities at home, Martha's grades were always excellent. Jerry Oppenheimer, in his book *Just Desserts*, writes that all the pressures of getting good grades, studying hard, and helping so much at home led Martha to develop lifelong personality traits. She became obsessive about cleanliness and was a perfectionist in nearly everything she did. She always tried to be absolutely correct and became an insomniac, going to sleep at 10:00 P.M. and rising at midnight to sit in the kitchen with her father, eating onion sandwiches, playing Scrabble, or talking for hours.[11]

Unlike her classmates at the elementary school who came only from Martha's neighborhood, students from all over Nutley attended Martha's junior high school. For the first time, she rubbed elbows with boys and girls from wealthier families whose parents were lawyers and executives. As with most girls her age, Martha, tall and thin with a wide smile and high cheekbones, was aware of her clothes; and, like other girls, she wanted to wear the latest fashions and have a closet filled with clothes like those her classmates were wearing. From mixing with students from families so different from her own, Martha developed an interest in social status. As she told her Aunt Estelle Burke, "When I grow up, I'm going to have three dogs and two maids to walk them."[12]

Martha was an avid reader, often spending time at the Nutley Public Library. Her mother gave approval for her to borrow books from the adult section, after Martha read everything that was offered on the shelves for her age level. About spending time at the library and reading, Martha once wrote, "my appetite for reading was whetted even further," adding that she loved reading Hawthorne, Austen, Dickens, Wharton, Tolstoy, Henry James, and George Eliot. She said, "Already curious about the writer's craft, I sought to discover the key to good literature, sometimes reading several books on the same subject just to figure out how one was better than the next."[13] And while Martha also read books that were popular for teens at the time, she didn't have teen idols, as many of her friends did. She didn't have posters on her bedroom walls or stacks of movie magazines in the closet.

Because she was expected to help with the household tasks, including preparing meals, her skills in the kitchen developed early. Like most young women in the 1950s, Martha and her female classmates took cooking classes in school. According to Jerry Oppenheimer, in *Just Desserts*, a junior high classmate of Martha's said that Martha, like most of her classmates, had little interest in cooking. She noted that cooking, or at least helping her mother cook, was one of Martha's chores at home, and that she had to do it or she would have gotten in trouble. Her classmate said that if home economics hadn't been mandatory, Martha wouldn't have gone near the classroom.[14]

Martha entered high school in 1956, the same year Elvis Presley debuted on *The Ed Sullivan Show*. Vowing to do her best in all her classes, she studied hard and, according to friends, often went over her notes until the minute before an exam. Barbara Viventi Howard, voted the girl "most likely to succeed" at Nutley High School, and who was later a prominent microbiologist, said there was certainly something extraordinary about Martha; she had a focus that was extremely unusual for Nutley High School girls of the 1950s. She added that Martha was highly ambitious and competitive.[15]

Martha joined the staff of the high school's literary quarterly, writing articles and book reviews. She was also an honors English student and elected to take four math courses rather than the required two, after being told by her father that she would need to earn her own way to college and not depend on him for college funds. By graduation, she had participated in more clubs than most of the other students. She also participated in the group that served hot dogs during the high school football games and was one of the coeds who participated in hosting one of the school's traditional before-game breakfasts that were served to the football team on Saturday mornings. She later described these events as her first catered party.

Martha graduated from Nutley High School in 1959. At the time, society and the family structure in America were changing. By the time she graduated from high school, she was part of the last of a generation that strictly valued a traditional family life and adhered to what authority figures espoused. For Martha and for most of her classmates, and certainly for her parents' generation in America, women worked in the home and valued the traditional family structure. As she left high school, however, culture and society were changing; and it was the young people, and those who were younger than Martha and her classmates, that were forcing the changes. They were challenging the status quo, using their creative minds and sometimes rebellious nature to ask questions, always looking for something different, and in many ways, questioning authority.

Martha and her classmates in the class of 1959 at Nutley High School was insulated from what was changing in America, and they didn't represent the changes seeping into society and culture. Christopher Byron writes in his book *Martha Inc.*, that only a few of the classmates in the class of 1959 seemed to sense what their future held or what opportunities awaited them. Vinny Cina, one of Martha's fellow students, described himself and his classmates as a close-knit group, without much influence from the outside world. Drugs and alcohol were around, he said, but they didn't know about such things yet. He said he and his classmates at Nutley High School were naive and, for the most part, were more focused on their studies.[16]

Byron also notes that although Martha belonged to the Nutley High School Honor Society, the Arts Committee, and various other committees and groups, she wasn't voted the cutest or the best looking or most talented or wittiest. She wasn't the most athletic or the friendliest or had the nicest smile or was the most likely to succeed. Rather, Martha was just one of the students, on one committee after the next. Many of the women who graduated from Nutley High School, including Martha, listed gardening, cooking, and homemaking as their interests. And most of these young women looked the same, wearing much the same hairdo, dressed in sweaters and pearls, and nearly all were white, of Irish, Polish, and Italian descent; most were Catholic. Author Byron writes that in her high school yearbook senior picture, Martha looked straight at the camera with a purposeful look, her large and serious face framed by tight bangs and curls that "reeked of motherly approval." The phrase beneath her picture reads: "I do what I please, and I do it with ease."[17] This sentiment, and others like it, seems to have been repeated by Martha many times over the years since 1959.

Despite the many changes in society and culture, Martha and the other graduates of 1959 had one foot in traditional American values of family, with the man the head of the household and the woman working in the home and raising the children, and the other foot ready to step into something very different. Martha was ready, however, to take her own steps, influenced by her father and her mother. Her father was demanding and her mother more passive. Her father was creative her mother more ordinary, managing the home and the family. Her father had high expectations, but her mother had few expectations at all. Although acknowledging that her father was a difficult and demanding man, Martha always said that he had a positive influence on her creativity. She only hinted about her father's strictness by stating, "My father took me under his wing, and I learned everything. He taught me how to garden, how to use all his tools. He helped me with public speaking. Mother may be the better teacher, because he taught by 'I'll beat it into you,' and mother did it in the more normal fashion. But I was receptive to that kind of teaching. I didn't mind at all."[18] Her brother Frank believed that because of his sister's perceptions and her treatment in her early life, likely from her father, that Martha became a man-hater, and that she didn't like male authority either growing up or as an adult.[19]

In her "Remembering" column in the December 1993 issue of *Martha Stewart Living*, Martha wrote that she owes her "self-confidence and self-worth" to her father. She added that he "drilled into my head on a regular basis" his credo, which she describes as "work hard, try hard, and most of your goals will be realized. Don't limit yourself."

One of the many ways Edward Kostyra influenced his daughter was by encouraging her to become a model. While in high school, Martha began working as a model at the famous Fifth Avenue department store, Bonwit Teller. Catching the bus into the city, Martha would leave school and go to her modeling job where she earned a great deal more than her classmates who had more conventional summer jobs. According to author Jerry Oppenheimer, in his book *Just Desserts*, Martha claimed she got into modeling after a neighborhood girl, already a model, introduced her to an agent. Her younger brother, Frank, remembers that it was their father who encouraged her. Frank said: "Dad pushed Martha into modeling . . . Martha was sort of reluctant, but Dad was a salesman. He could see that Martha's looks had a retail value and he wanted to market them. He had a Rolleiflex and a darkroom, and he took hundreds of photographs of her. She spent hours posing for him: 'Smile . . . turn your face that way . . . turn your face this way . . . the light's not right . . . wait for the light!'"[20]

The modeling world in New York was enlightening to Martha, a young woman from the working-class community of Nutley, New Jersey. It was a powerful world that surprised her, challenged her, and, at the same time, made her fearful and wanting more. One powerful agent, notes Jerry Oppenheimer in *Just Desserts,* suggested that she needed to lose her classic features and look more like Twiggy, a popular, pencil-thin British model of the time. He also suggested that she should have her teeth pulled to provide the effect of sunken cheeks, and then wear false teeth when she wasn't modeling.

A Manhattan modeling agency signed Martha as a client. In the January 28, 1991 edition of *New York* magazine, Martha wrote, "I remember modeling at Bonwit Teller on Saturdays. They had these little girls modeling these high-fashion dresses. I can remember thinking I should probably be at the football game or something. But it was fun."[21] The agency sent her on a casting call and she was chosen to appear in a soup commercial, which ran during a popular prime-time television show. While her wholesome, classic look was in demand, Martha's New Jersey accent was not. To remedy the problem, the producers of the commercials dubbed her voice with one that was easier on the ear. A classmate, Barbara Rubin Oliver, said of Martha at the time: "In Nutley in those days we all talked fast and talked New Jersey talk—Martha included. Back then Martha didn't have that wonderful kind of WASPy way of speaking that she developed later when she created herself. Now she articulates. Her speech patterns were different back then. That's why I get a kick out of watching her on TV now."[22]

While it was her father who pushed her into modeling, it was Martha who turned it into an advantage, however, her busy school and modeling schedule left little time for boys. This lack of interest in a social life was also likely due to her father-daughter relationship and family problems. Also, Martha herself was very goal oriented and had a strong a drive to succeed. According to high school friends who remembered her during her high school years, although Martha had a strong will and wanted desperately to succeed in all that she was involved in, Edward was very strict and didn't like any of the boys Martha went out with. He believed a steady boyfriend would take her away from what was important— succeeding in high school and going on to college.

Author Lloyd Allen, in his book *Being Martha,* notes that, as a teenager, Martha never went through an awkward phase. Although she was beautiful, hard work, not beauty, was valued in the Kostyra household. Martha Sr. described her oldest daughter during her high school days as being very studious, spending much of her time in the library. Her mother said that Martha read a lot, did her homework, was a part of committees at school including working on the prom, and was an all around student who always tried to excel. Martha, her mother said, was always on the honor roll and no one had to encourage her to study. She was so busy in school that she didn't have very many dates, but certainly she wasn't intimidated by boy; she may have put any romance on the back burner.[23]

By the time Martha was a senior at Nutley High School, her hard work, participating in groups and on committees, and her good grades had paid off. She earned a partial scholarship to Barnard College, one of the nation's finest women's colleges. In *New York Magazine*, Martha wrote, "I had little choice of where I could go to college because I had to live at home. NYU gave me a full scholarship. Barnard offered me only a very partial scholarship, but I was modeling and I knew I could make enough money to pay for my education, so I chose Barnard."[24]

Martha's friends, however, weren't aware that she had a choice of schools or that she had been awarded a full scholarship to New York University. In their opinion, Edward Kostyra would have demanded that she accepted the full tuition scholarship, rather than the partial scholarship at Barnard. Yet, Martha's mother stated that her daughter had been such a good student that New York University did indeed offer her a full scholarship. She remembers a meeting with the high school principal who advised that, because Martha had been accepted at Barnard, that school would be a better school for her.[25] It was because of this advice and despite a full scholarship that Martha enrolled at Barnard College for Women.

By the time Martha was ready to enter college and eager for what was ahead, many factors influenced what she believed and how she intended to live her life: her parents, siblings, her Polish heritage, the working class community of Nutley, and the society and culture of the 1940s and 1950s. And it was all of this, and what came next—college, continuing her modeling career, and marriage—that also greatly influenced her and prepared her for what she would eventually become, one of the most successful businesswomen in America. In later years, many women didn't typically list such interests as gardening, homemaking, and cooking in their yearbook pictures. Instead they began to break out culturally and professionally, and didn't strictly follow what their mothers did or their fathers expected. However, it isn't surprising that the interests Martha and her classmates in the late 1950s listed were exactly what she later turned into a very successful business empire.

NOTES

1. Jerry Oppenheimer, *Just Desserts* (Boca Raton: American Media, 1997), 35.

2. Martha Stewart, *Weddings* (New York: Clarkson N. Potter, 1999), 8.

3. Christopher Byron, *Martha Inc.* (New York: John Wiley & Sons, 2003), 35.

4. Martha Stewart, *Martha Stewart's New Old House* (New York: Clarkson N. Potter, 1992), 9.

5. Lloyd Allen, *Being Martha* (New Jersey: John Wiley & Sons, 2006), 38.

6. Ibid., 38–39, 41.

7. Byron, *Martha Inc.*, 33.

8. Martha Stewart, *Martha Stewart's Gardening* (New York: Clarkson N. Potter, 1991), 5, 41.

9. Martha Stewart, *Martha Stewart's Pies and Tarts* (New York: Clarkson N. Potter, 1985), 1, 2.

10. Allen, *Being Martha*, 40.

11. Oppenheimer, *Just Desserts*, 62.

12. Ibid., 63.

13. Martha Stewart, "Remembering," *Martha Stewart Living*, October and November 1993.

14. Oppenheimer, *Just Desserts*, 65.

15. Ibid., 67.

16. Byron, *Martha Inc.*, 43.

17. Ibid., 44–45.

18. Ibid., 53–54.

19. Ibid., 54.

20. Oppenheimer, *Just Desserts*, 71.

21. Ibid., 73.

22. Ibid.

23. Allen, *Being Martha*, 46.

24. Oppenheimer, *Just Desserts*, 82.

25. Allen, *Being Martha*, 48, 49.

Chapter 3

COLLEGE, MODELING, AND MARRIAGE

We were brought up unpretentiously but with a lot of spirit and a lot of "you can do anything you want to do" hammered into our heads.

—Martha Stewart

I do what I please, and I do it with ease.
—Martha Stewart's senior class picture inscription,
Nutley High School, 1959

In the fall of 1959, Martha Kostyra Stewart entered Barnard College for Women in New York City. This was a time of great change in America, with social upheaval at home and a war in Southeast Asia. It was also a time that many consider to be the decade of America's youth, for the first wave of baby boomers, those born between 1946 and 1964, became old enough to attend college and serve in the military. More individuals than ever before came of age in the 1960s, and everyday life brought both increased comforts and growing social challenges.

In the early 1960s, unlike in previous decades, the economy was more urban than rural centered, and there were various "movements" afoot, such as increased rights for women and for minorities. As Martha entered college, a broad range of changes in society and culture was taking hold in the areas of sexual standards, drug use, and radically different clothing styles. This was a change from prior decades where a more conservative lifestyle was the norm. Instead, it was a time where sexual freedoms, including premarital sex, multiple sexual relationships, and unmarried couples living together, put a strain on families and on the general public. Many parents found increased drug use and changes in sexual mores difficult to tolerate or even accept. For many in America, moral and religious issues were often at the heart of growing conflicts within families and in society. All this surrounded Martha as a new college student at Barnard College for Women.

There were also significant advances in educational opportunities. For the first time, a growing number of young men and women entered higher education degree programs; this trend continued throughout the decade. College campuses all across America became the center for at least a part of a growing revolution that concerned civil rights, antiwar activities, and changing moral behaviors and religious practices.

At Barnard College, a part of the Columbia University campus, many students joined in peace marches and rallies to protest segregation. Many also took part in greater sexual freedoms and expressed what was considered radical political views on other issues of the day. Yet while all of this swirled around Martha, she didn't take part in any of these activities. Just as in high school, she was driven to succeed academically and had little time for anything else. As a freshman studying art history, to save money she enrolled at Barnard as a day student, commuting from her home in Nutley, New Jersey. Her time was always at a premium. Along with studying to earn good grades, she continued her part-time modeling career for the Fifth Avenue Bonwit Teller department store. For Martha, earning an income was necessary, as this was what in part enabled her to attend college.

Studying hard to earn excellent grades was natural for Martha, yet college was a new experience. At Barnard, the high academic standards and the intellectual requirements were somewhat overwhelming, however, because Martha's roots were in a working-class neighborhood where many young people were not able to go to college. As a freshman, Martha was required to take five courses per semester at this competitive school where students rarely received As for their work. All of this, combined with a daily commute from her parents' home and her part-time modeling job, made for a hectic life, with little time for a social life or for taking part in any of the activities on or off campus.

Martha's days were filled with studying, work, attending classes, and commuting; and she found that she required little sleep, had a great amount of energy, and thrived on the stresses of her hectic life. This was a prediction of what her life would always be like—that of an achiever, perhaps an overachiever, and a woman constantly at a fast pace and always determined to succeed.

After one semester as a commuting student, Martha decided to move away from home and obtained a position through the college's student placement as a live-in housekeeper for two women who lived on Fifth Avenue. Her duties included cooking, cleaning, and running errands in exchange for meals and a weekly salary. Her daily commute to campus was shorter, but her focus remained on her college classes and on her modeling career. She obtained more modeling jobs at Bendel's and Bergdorf's, both prominent New York City department stores at the time. In college, just as in high school, Martha went out on only a few dates. Sometimes her classmates arranged for her to meet eligible young men, and any dates that she did have as a college freshman were often the result of her attending college mixers, parties that were popular at the time. Although premarital sex and experimenting with drugs were prevalent at the time, Martha didn't participate as did many of her classmates. It may have been her strict Catholic upbringing or her drive to succeed, or it may have been her hectic, demanding schedule that kept her from experimenting with sex and drugs; it may also have been the result of her father's influence.

According to Jerry Oppenheimer in his book, *Just Desserts*, a friend of Martha's during her freshman and sophomore years at Barnard College attributed her sexual conservatism to her religious beliefs and to her high personal goals. She described Martha as very picky and choosy about men. Martha, she said, thought the other girls would go out with just anyone, and she believed that one should be more discriminating. Oppenheimer writes that according to Martha's college friend, Martha didn't date at all, and that other girls were often experimenting with their personal freedom, but Martha did not. She believed that girls were less desirable if they experimented sexually just to get a date or to be considered popular. Rather, Martha was convinced she would be popular without such behavior and that in Martha's view, first you were engaged and then you were married.[1]

Another friend from Barnard agreed. She stated that it was Martha's intention to marry well. "She knew what was available in the world, and she wanted to get some of that for herself...Martha wanted somebody who was rich, who would give her a certain kind of lifestyle. She knew what she wanted, and she wasn't going to take any risks to not achieve her goals. That was obvious."[2]

In August 1960, Martha was selected by *Glamour* magazine as one of the 10 best-dressed college girls in America. *Glamour*, at the time, was one of the nation's leading fashion magazines, and the announcement appeared in the popular annual back-to-school edition in 1961. Believing she had the potential to be chosen, Martha had submitted her application that included photos of her wearing casual and business style clothing, some of which she had borrowed from friends. According to Jerry Oppenheimer, in *Just Desserts*, *Glamour*'s announcement included a full-page photograph of Martha wearing a coat, gloves, heels, and carrying an alligator bag, and described her as a young woman of "tenderness" and "vitality." The magazine described Martha as having an expressive face, and that "life pleases her...in particular, a young man named Andy, art and architecture...she cooks, too."[3]

According to author Oppenheimer, Barbara Stone, *Glamour*'s editor at the time, and in later years, Martha's agent, said the magazine's contest was very important in those years and that many young women wanted to win it. Colleges all over the country were hoping to have their coeds selected as a best-dressed college girl. When Martha entered the competition, she was ahead of the other competitors because she had already been a model, giving her important experience and perhaps a leg up on all the others vying to win.[4]

At the time of her application for this prestigious honor, Martha was planning her wedding to Andy Stewart. She knew being selected would be a boost to her modeling career and was also an honor for Barnard College. Knowing it might diminish her chances in being selected, her application for the *Glamour* magazine award did not include her marriage plans.

ANDY STEWART

Andy Stewart was born in New York City on February 8, 1938. His parents, George and Ethel Stewart, were considered a worldly couple who traveled the globe, often moving their family from place to place. George Stewart was seemingly obsessed by travel and if he heard about an interesting place to visit or to live, he would travel there or even move the family to live there. As a result, Andy found himself never in one place long enough to have an organized education. As a result, much of his life was full of commotion and upheaval.

George Stewart came from a large Jewish family. His parents, who had emigrated from Russia, adhered to strict Jewish traditions. George, a stock trader, owned a seat on the New York Stock Exchange during the 1950s. He often gave friends and acquaintances the impression that he was well to do, especially because of his world travels and his Wall Street connections. Ethel Stewart, Andy's mother, was an outspoken woman and an obsessive home decorator. According to author Jerry Oppenheimer, a family friend described Ethel Stewart as someone who loved decorating, stating she once even purchased an apartment just to redecorate it, but not to live in it.[5] In an article that appeared in the October 7, 1991 issue of *New York* magazine, Ethel Stewart declared that other than her family, there was nothing as important to her as her homes and that she was very comfortable with grandeur.[6]

Ethel Stewart thought travel was important to her children's education. She also felt traveling and living in faraway places was her opportunity to polish her decorating skills. In the same issue of *New York* magazine, Ethel Stewart stated that she never wanted to copy anyone when decorating and that she valued originality. She went on to say that when they were traveling, they always had to stay at the Plaza Athenee, an expensive and famous hotel, not just for days or weeks, but for months at a time.[7]

Many recall Ethel Stewart as bossy, but others recall her more warmly. According to Christopher Byron in his book *Martha Inc.*, a friend remembered Ethel as a slim, gracious woman with deep religious beliefs and someone who often dressed like a 1920s era flapper.[8] Another described Andy's mother as a woman who wanted everything in the world to be perfect and would become quite agitated and concerned if she thought someone might be suffering over something and added that they admired her very much.[9] George Stewart was a nonpracticing Jew despite being from a large and devout Jewish family; Ethel Stewart was a devoted Christian Scientist.

After spending his middle-school years at a school in New York State, Andy Stewart spent his high school years at Putney School in Vermont, a school with a working farm where he learned to work the land, the construction trades, and where he acquired various farm skills. He graduated from Putney in June 1955 and, although he had set his sites on attending Harvard, he instead attended the University of Virginia. Because of his broadminded and permissive upbringing that included traveling the world and parents who expected him to be independent, Andy felt out of place on campus. Whereas the majority of his classmates were conservative in their views, Andy was a civil rights activist; whereas many of his fellow students dressed in jackets and ties, he preferred working-style clothing.

Realizing that his schooling at Putney left him without some of the academic skills he needed in college and wanting to succeed at the university, Andy settled in to work hard, despite his philosophical and external differences. He began taking courses in philosophy after developing an interest in cosmology, the philosophical study and explanation of the nature of the universe. For his honors program, he wrote a thesis on human equality. In June 1959, as a member of several honor societies, he graduated with a degree in philosophy and a Phi Beta Kappa key. At the time of his graduation, the military draft, which nearly guaranteed being sent to Southeast Asia, was on the minds of every man Andy's age. Realizing he must stay in school to avoid the draft, he applied and was accepted into the law program at Yale.

In the spring of 1960, during an art class, Diane Stewart Love, an art major at Barnard, noticed Martha, a tall, slim, blond sophomore, entering an art classroom. Diane was always looking for someone to introduce to her brother, Andy Stewart. She approached Martha, told her she had a very nice brother, and asked if she might be interested in meeting him. Martha gave Diane her phone number and after a phone call from Andy, the two agreed to meet. On the evening of their first date, when Andy first saw Martha Kostyra, he was glad he had taken his sister's advice and had called the lovely blond. There were several subsequent dates and before long, the two couldn't bear to be apart. In a January 1991 interview in *New York* magazine, Martha stated that she and Andy fell in love on the first date and that Andy was shocked that she always accepted every invitation for a date. She added that since she hadn't read any F. Scott Fitzgerald novels, she didn't know that girls were supposed to lead men on.[10]

During the summer of 1960, Andy left on a trip abroad, something he had longed planned, and Martha continued her employment as a housekeeper. When he returned, the two dated again and in the fall, Andy went back to Yale and his law studies. Martha returned to her studies at Barnard. She continued modeling and her housekeeping duties and before long, Martha made weekend trips to New Haven to see Andy. Shortly thereafter they became lovers and their relationship reached a new level. According to friends, it was obvious the two loved each other. A friend of Martha's said that she was concerned about the turn the relationship had taken, and said that Martha never stopped talking about it, and there was a lot of emotion. There was also fear, but that she felt good and bad all at the same time. Martha, her friend added, was worried about pregnancy and also that maybe she really didn't love Andy and had gone way too far with him. Another concern was how her father would feel about her dating or what he would do if he ever found out about her love affair with Andy.[11] Martha was a strict Catholic, brought up in a strict religious household. As well, she was raised in a different spiritual and intellectual environment than Andy. Despite their religious and philosophical differences, the two continued their relationship.

In late 1960, Martha and Andy went to Nutley to visit her family. It was the first time he had met any members of the Kostyra family. Martha's mother and siblings welcomed Andy to the family home, but Martha's father, Edward, was upset that his oldest daughter was dating and possibly in love. He looked for excuses to criticize Andy and his feelings caused a fight within the Kostyra family. George Kostyra, Martha's youngest brother, said it was an interesting meeting, describing Andy as a preppie dressed in coveralls, someone who liked to use his hands. "It was a great fit, because that's the way we were. We were the same as everybody else on the street—working families—but somehow my father thought we had an aristocratic background. I remember Andy asking my father for my sister's hand in marriage. We were all huddled in the kitchen with our ears to the door wondering what was going on."[12]

Martha Sr. said that Andy fit in very well with her family. And, like a member of the family, he would take part in the blessing of the eggs at Easter time and he would wish everyone good luck and good health, just like the rest of her family. She added: "Martha was rather young compared to today's brides, but I always had the feeling that she knew what she was doing."[13]

Believing that Andy Stewart was from an affluent family, Martha thought marrying him would bring the wealth and the lifestyle she had always wanted. Andy was considered handsome; he was enrolled at Yale, a very prestigious school; and his parents were seemingly wealthy, as they were well traveled and sophisticated and lived in a large apartment in Manhattan. All this was a lifestyle not at all like what Martha knew, but one she had often dreamed about as she grew up in Nutley, New Jersey.

MARRIAGE

Andy proposed marriage in February 1961. Martha told Andy she was too young to be married, that he was too young as well, and that she wanted to continue her modeling career. Martha's modeling career, particularly as a result of the *Glamour* magazine award, was moving along and she felt there was a chance she could go to Paris to model for a French magazine. Andy worried that if Martha went to Paris, he might never see her again. In an article that appeared in *People* magazine in April 1980, Andy said, "We were young and innocent. We never had the experience we might have had if we married four or five years later. But Martha might have changed and I would not have wanted her." In the same article, Martha said that Andy had come to the city from New Haven and she mentioned the Paris possibility, stating, "He stood outside my window throwing stones at one in the morning. Finally I snuck out of the dorm in my bathrobe. He drove around and around Central Park telling me I should marry him."[14]

By this time, Martha had left her position as a housekeeper and moved to a building on the Columbia University campus. A few weeks later, she said yes to the marriage proposal and in early March 1961, the two were engaged. At the news of the engagement, Edward Kostyra was furious, stating that marriage would ruin Martha's chances of success and used himself as an example of how marriage can damage someone's potential. In the April 1980 issue of *People* magazine, Martha said that her father told her she was crazy, but that she decided to go ahead because she thought Andy was honest and also that he was very serious.[15]

Martha's father was also against the marriage because Andy wasn't Catholic. Lloyd Allen, in the book *Being Martha*, says that Martha Sr. believed that Andy was attracted to her daughter's intelligence and her diligence. She believed her daughter was attracted to Andy's romantic nature, and Martha Sr. had no objection to Andy, even though he was Jewish. She knew Andy's mother was a Christian Scientist and that his father was Jewish, but not observant, and that she felt they were nice people. She said her family accepted Andy's parents even though they were different and she felt the Stewarts accepted Martha and they regarded her very highly.[16]

Andy's Jewish roots were not a concern for the couple. In the 1996 winter-spring *Martha Stewart Living* special weddings issue, Martha wrote that her family cheerfully included Andy in their holiday celebrations and that she enjoyed being a part of his family's observances. She added that with the exception of Andy's mother, his family did not practice their religion.[17] And Judaism wasn't part of their lives later in their marriage. In her *Remembering* column, in the December 1992 and January 1993 issue of *Martha Stewart Living,* Martha wrote, "We decided to raise (Alexis, their daughter) in no single religion but to educate her on all of them. We invented our own holiday rituals and, as time went on, they became important to me...family gatherings have become the central holiday rituals, the cornerstones of our lives."[18]

On July 1, 1961, in a simple ceremony held at the St. Paul's Chapel at Columbia University, with only immediate family members as witnesses, Martha Kostyra married Andy Stewart. But Martha kept Andy waiting at the altar. In a March 1987 issue of *USA Today Weekend,* Martha described the ceremony, saying that she was late and that her father was nervous. She said Andy was waiting for her while the wedding music was played over and over, and that she was just procrastinating before she walked down the aisle.[19]

About the marriage Martha Sr. said: "Maybe she was too young; I don't know. But Martha always seemed so mature, and you hesitated to give her any advice because she thought she knew it all. She fell like a ton of bricks. He had a lot of exposure; he was worldly, his father was a stockbroker, and his mother taught Martha a lot about antiques. Everybody loved him. He was someone who could fit right in. He liked to fit in and please. You had the feeling that he related to you, and he did. No airs."[20]

Remembering her wedding day, Martha Stewart wrote in the preface of her book *Weddings*, published in 1987, that there was little time and no money for her wedding. She stated, "I was a naïve nineteen-year-old... our families were somewhat overcome at the prospect of our marriage, but we were strong-willed enough to just go off and do it." She wrote that she and her mother made her dress and saved enough of the fabric to cover a pillbox hat, like the one Jackie Kennedy wore. For her wedding bouquet, she carried field daisies, and instead of invitations, she wrote cards to the family. She added, "I suppose it was very basic, but I didn't feel that way. I felt very special.[21]

After their brief honeymoon, the Stewarts returned to work. Martha continued to work as a model and Andy had a summer job as a law clerk for a New York law firm. They spent the summer at a penthouse apartment, lent to them by a friend. In the fall, they rented a home situated on 30 acres just outside of Guilford, Connecticut, near New Haven and Yale Law School so that Andy could finish his third year of law school. Like so many other women at the time, Martha put her own education on hold, intending to return to Barnard to finish her undergraduate degree in the future.

In June 1962, Andy graduated from Yale Law School and the couple returned to New York City. They rented a small apartment near the Columbia University campus that a friend described as a miserable place, complete with roaches, an apartment that Martha absolutely hated.[22] The apartment had three rooms and their neighbors were a mix of blue-collar workers and university people. Years later, Martha still had bad memories of the Manhattan apartment. In his book *Just Desserts*, Jerry Oppenheimer says that when she was giving a lecture at the Boston Junior League, Martha responded to an audience question about how her elegant lifestyle could relate to someone living in a one-room apartment. Martha was visibly irritated and responded, "When I was your age I lived in three *miserable* rooms overlooking the rooftops of 114th Street, and I still had time to plant some herbs on my windowsill, and still had time to go around to junk shops and collect some pretty things. And I made my life nicer. I worked for everything I have. I'm 20 years older than you are. Can't you see that?"[23]

Martha apparently did like something about the first apartment she shared with her new husband in New York. In a February-March 1993 "Remembering" column in *Martha Stewart Living* magazine, she wrote that the bathtub was so long enough that she could lie down in it, and that the pedestal sink was so big that she could arrange pretty bowls that held her cotton balls and Q-tips.[24]

In the fall of 1962, Andy enrolled in a graduate program at Columbia for a master of law degree and worked part-time for a law firm. Martha resumed her studies at Barnard and continued her modeling career. By this time, Andy and Martha began traveling the Northeast looking for farm property. Under the guidance of Andy's mother, they also developed a great interest in antiques and spent many weekends attending auctions and visiting antique shops.

Martha's sister Laura remembered the frequent trips, stating that antiquing was a big family activity and that Andy's mother educated Martha about antiques. Martha, she added, wanted to have antiques right away. At the time, they were affordable and fit with Andy and Martha's budget. Once a month, the Stewart's would go to Nyack, New York for an auction. As they walked around previewing what was up for auction, Martha would pick out a piece and a short while later, it would appear in their home. Bidding at auctions started early in Martha's life, thanks in part to the teachings of Ethel Stewart, and now, Laura said, her sister bids at Sotheby's auctions and has a lot more money to spend.[25]

In January 1964, Andy finished his graduate degree studies and Martha had one paper to write to fulfill the requirements of a bachelor's of arts degree. To celebrate both their achievements, the couple decided to take a trip to Europe. On their return, Martha finished the required course work and graduated from Barnard in June 1964 with a degree in art history. Andy started work at a law firm and began studying for the bar exam, and Martha devoted her time to her modeling career. The couple rented a six-room apartment with a river view at $250 per month. This sum was much more than they could afford at the time; however, both were confident that they could earn high enough salaries to enable them to pay the rent on a home where they both believed they should live. Life moved along for the couple as they enjoyed living and working in the city they loved.

Despite Martha's determination to continue her modeling career, her opportunities began to dwindle. One reason may have been the move away from New York, the center of the modeling world, to New Haven so that Andy could complete his law degree at Yale. It may also have been because the "look" that modeling agencies and advertisers were seeking was changing. Now the required "look" was thin, nearly gaunt models, wearing skimpier clothes, giving the impression of a lifestyle far different than what Martha portrayed. For her part, Martha never accepted that what she had to offer—her tall, lean, polished, natural look, popular during her high school and college days—wasn't in demand any longer. She had always dreamed of a being a famous model, walking the long runways of the high fashion world, complete with the fame and money that accompanied success. With these dreams in hand, she had even flown to Paris to seek modeling jobs and gain exposure in the high fashion world. After a month there, she hadn't landed sufficient modeling work and returned to the United States. Discouraged by the experience, she remained determined to succeed in New York.

In early 1965, when Martha was 23 years old, she discovered she was pregnant. The pregnancy wasn't planned, although according to Martha Sr., both Martha and Andy were thrilled with the news, even though it was still Martha's intention to continue her dream of walking the runways of the great designers as a famous model. Telling her friends and family she was excited about the prospect of having a child, Martha began preparing for her baby. On September 27, 1965, Alexis Gilbert Stewart was born. Although the couple's life changed dramatically, and despite not getting as many modeling jobs as she wanted, Martha was determined to continue modeling. She also decided to begin entertaining on a level she had always dreamed about.

NOTES

1. Jerry Oppenheimer, *Just Desserts* (Boca Raton: American Media, 2003), 92–93.
2. Ibid., 93.
3. Ibid., 90.
4. Ibid.
5. Ibid.
6. Ibid., 98.
7. Ibid., 99.
8. Christopher Byron, *Martha Inc.* (New York: John Wiley & Sons, 2003), 51.
9. Ibid.
10. Oppenheimer, *Just Desserts*, 103.
11. Ibid., 105.
12. Lloyd Allen, *Being Martha* (New Jersey: John Wiley & Sons, 2006), 51.
13. Ibid., 51–52.
14. Oppenheimer, *Just Desserts*, 108.
15. Ibid., 109.
16. Allen, *Being Martha*, 50.
17. Oppenheimer, *Just Desserts*, 111.
18. Ibid., 111.
19. Ibid., 114.
20. Allen, *Being Martha*, 50.
21. Martha Stewart, *Weddings* (New York: Clarkson N. Potter, 1987), viii–ix.
22. Oppenheimer, *Just Desserts*, 119.
23. Ibid., 120.
24. Ibid.
25. Allen, *Being Martha*, 57.

Chapter 4

MOTHERHOOD, A MOVE TO WESTPORT, AND A NEW CAREER

They were good parents. They never didn't have time to explain something. That's how I raised my daughter, Alexis, too. And that's what I hope the American family could be and should be: busy and happy and everybody helping each other.

—Martha Stewart

Before Martha became pregnant, the Stewarts had discussed starting a family, although they hadn't yet decided to commit to the idea or begin planning. On hearing the news that she would have a baby in September 1965, both Andy and Martha quickly decided it was time to renovate, decorate, and furnish a baby's room in their New York City apartment. Some friends noted that this part of preparing for a new baby was exactly what Martha delighted in; she loved decorating, planning the color schemes, and determining exactly what was just right for the baby's arrival. After an uncomplicated pregnancy, Alexis Gilbert Stewart was born on September 27, 1965. The new baby was named after Martha's paternal grandmother, and Martha and Andy decided to call her Lexi.

Soon after Lexi was born, Martha and Andy purchased a nineteenth-century schoolhouse near Middlefield, Massachusetts, located in the western part of the state in the foothills of the Berkshire Mountains. Their new home, which they intended to use on the weekends, had no running water or plumbing; water for washing and cooking had to be hauled from a nearby stream. The home, purchased with all of their savings, was named Middlefield. It took Martha and Andy, nearly five years to complete the renovation, doing most of the work themselves and working on it nearly every weekend. Martha has written about the long and difficult renovation many times over the years. In her book *Martha Stewart's Quick Cook*, she writes: "Andy learned carpentry, plumbing, ditch digging...I became an excellent house painter, landscape architect, iron-stove chef and basic jack-of-all trades. Every Sunday evening we lugged back bushels of fresh produce for ourselves and our friends in New York."[1]

Purchasing the old schoolhouse was a dream and a nightmare for the couple; neither of them understood the amount of work involved in a renovation, or the time it would take to complete the work. Neither was aware of the toll it would take on them physically, on their relationship, and their family life. Nearly every weekend, the couple loaded up their old Mercedes for the 400-mile round trip drive from the city to work on the home, leaving on Friday evening and returning on Sunday night. Both felt pressure to get the project finished, to say nothing of completing it to their expected level of perfection, and much of the time they were at odds with regard to what should be done and how it should be accomplished.

Soon after Lexi was born, Martha returned to work. With the help of a new housekeeper and baby-sitting assistance from a budding actress who lived in the same apartment building, she was determined to resume her modeling career and went looking for jobs. At the time, a highly regarded photographer, Paul Elfenbein, was doing a series of photographs of young mothers and their babies for the Johnson & Johnson Company. Combing through photographs of models, his production assistant, Kathy Tatlock, found a photograph of Martha and was taken by her smile and her natural look. She was delighted when she found out that this tall slender beauty also had a young daughter, and she contacted Martha about the photo shoot. In his book *Just Desserts*, Tatlock said that they called Martha in for some photo test shots and that Martha was excited about the job because it paid well and was for Johnson & Johnson. Oppenheimer notes that the ad people loved Martha's looks for the ad; however, they were less than enchanted by Lexi. Tatlock said that Lexi had wonderful features, but that she was odd-looking, like a puppy with wrinkles. She said they decided Lexi wasn't the ideal Johnson & Johnson baby, one with blue eyes and blonde hair.[2] To Martha's disappointment, the job went to another mother and daughter team. Martha's determination to be a top model, walking the runways for famous designers and commanding top money was fading. The realization that now top models were taller, thinner, and often looked more exotic than the look she offered was something she realized and accepted, difficult as it was for her.

In the meantime, Martha and Andy were working every weekend on the Middlefield home. Martha decided that instead of modeling, she would hone her cooking and entertaining skills. After all, she loved entertaining and for several years had hosted many parties for family and friends. She realized that it was the actual presentation of her home, her family, and good food that was important to her. She knew it was important to others as well.

To help with this new direction in her life, Martha referred to the experts in the field; one of them was the celebrated chef Julia Child. In 1961, Child's book *Mastering the Art of French Cooking* was published to great fanfare. Like many who wanted to emulate the famous chef, Martha became a disciple. In her book *Entertaining*, she told her readers: "At home, like all my contemporaries, I had Julia Child's *Mastering the Art of French Cooking* in hand, and worked my way through from cover to cover. Julia brought calm into the realm of haute cuisine and inspired confidence. I was determined to try everything."[3]

A few years later, when Martha opened her catering business, Julia Child became an important mentor, although Martha did not get to know her personally until years later. Martha devoured Child's cookbooks long before she met her. She taught herself the art of French cuisine by preparing every one of her recipes in *Mastering the Art of French Cooking*. The recipes became the basis for her deep interest in food from around the world. Martha's father was her first mentor, a man who loved growing tomatoes and other fresh vegetables and flowers in a backyard garden, but in Julia Child, Martha found another mentor from whom she could learn the art of French cooking.

At their apartment in Manhattan on Riverside Drive, Martha began giving cocktail and dinner parties for friends, family, and Andy's colleagues at the law firm. Over time, many of the parties became extravagant events including 80 or 90 people. In December 1965, Martha hosted her biggest party ever. The invitations stated, "Christmas Carols, Cocktails and Desserts" and Martha spent weeks planning the event that was meant to celebrate the holiday and to also welcome their new daughter into the world.

Martha soon became known for her theme parties and, as she became more experienced with cooking, she began entertaining on a regular basis. At these events, many of the guests often discussed the issues of the day including the turmoil that seemed to be affecting so much of life during the tumultuous mid-1960s. While Andy would engage in heated discussions about the Vietnam War, Martha wasn't interested in any issues of the day. Although she was known as smart and ambitious, and could easily discuss any events she wished to, she wasn't interested in the intellectual or political issues of the day. Instead, she preferred to use her time to further her own career and that of her husband; to her it was the parties she hosted, the food she offered, and the presentation of it all that were important. She loved to have fun and enjoyed entertaining.

MARTHA STEWART AS STOCKBROKER ON WALL STREET

By the time Lexi was a toddler, Martha decided she needed another career. Although she didn't want to give up her parties and entertaining, she realized having an income was important. Andy was working for a law firm and earning a good salary; however, if they were to live the lifestyle that was important to them, Martha decided they needed more money. The idea that she could use her entertaining and presentation skills, along with her gardening and decorating expertise, didn't occur to her until much later. What did appeal to her at the time was the financial world of Wall Street. Earning a high salary became important and by this time she had realized it wasn't Andy's family, or any potential inheritance from his parents, that was going to provide them the means to live as she had always dreamed, which was the lifestyle of wealthy New Yorkers with a home in the country and an apartment in the city. Selling stocks and bonds and the money that could be made on Wall Street beckoned.

In August 1968, when she turned 27 years old, Martha passed the securities exam and was hired by Andy Monness of Monness, Williams & Sidel. Whether it was her need or her hunger for a high salary, or the fact that Andy's father, George Stewart, encouraged her to become a stockbroker like himself, Martha turned to the aggressive, fast-paced world of finance and Wall Street. According to Jerry Oppenheimer, in the book *Just Desserts*, a friend arranged for Martha to meet with Andy Monness. Remembering his first meeting with Martha, he said that Martha amazed him with her beauty and brains. He added that she made a winning impression right away, and that she was articulate. He believed Martha could sell anything.[4] Andy Monness made the easy decision to hire Martha.

At the time of her hire, Monness, Williams & Sidel had been in business only three years. Because it was a relatively new firm, and not one of the old, established Wall Street firms where clients typically felt more comfortable doing business, the firm was aggressive and hungry to succeed. They hired individuals who fit this mold. Martha was driven and assertive, and her first mentor, her father, had taught her about selling. As Martha began her career as a stockbroker, there weren't yet many women in the workforce. Most of her contemporaries were homemakers. In the securities industry, there were even fewer women. Adding to this hurdle, it was the late 1960s, turbulent years in America and the world. There was political turmoil surrounding the Vietnam War and the Martin Luther King and Bobby Kennedy assassinations, and there were anti-war demonstrations and civil rights marches and rallies around the country. Because of all of these factors, Wall Street suffered many ups and downs and it was an uneasy time for investors. For anyone to be successful in this highly competitive industry, especially at this time, it took hard work, risk, and dedication. It also took excellent sales skills, a dedication to detail, and an aggressive attitude. For women, it was even more difficult to succeed, but Martha possessed all the correct and useful attributes and turned being a woman in a male-dominated industry into a plus, rather than a detriment.

Despite all the volatility, politically and socially, and in spite of having a young daughter, another unusual characteristic for working women of the day. Martha was one of the top earners at the firm within two years. In her popular book, *Martha Stewart's Quick Cook,* published in 1983, Martha wrote about being a stockbroker while maintaining a home, saying that she was always faced with the daily challenge of cooking something that her husband and daughter would find interesting. She said cooking meals when she returned home late in the afternoon became a type of game to her where she would find ways to cook creatively after spending as little time as possible shopping. She found ways to cook healthful meals quickly by developing ways to simplify recipes without sacrificing taste and quality. She wrote: "I never got into the habit of freezing casseroles or fresh meats and fishes for future thawing. I never bought an unripe tomato with the idea that it would be ready to eat in five days...I was brought up in a large family where meal preparation was often an all day affair—inexpensive cuts of meats were braised or stewed to make them more palatable."[5] She added that when she was a stockbroker on Wall Street, she often entertained clients by taking them to lunch or dinner at some of the best restaurants in New York. She said she was introduced to *haute cuisine* in those fancy kitchens. When enjoying something especially delicious, she would often ask about the recipe or the ingredients and then create the recipe at home for her family.[6]

With Martha earning a six-figure salary and Andy's successful law career, the couple's income offered them the lifestyle that Martha had always dreamed of. While their careers seemed to be going along as both had planned, their schedules were rigorous. It wasn't long before both were exhausted. Their jobs were stressful and both felt pressured to succeed.

In early 1970, Andy had left the law firm and joined the legal department of Bangor Punta Corporation where he was required to learn a new area of the law as a corporate attorney. Martha felt pressure to recommend the right stocks and sell securities to make commissions.

MOVING TO WESTPORT AND TURKEY HILL FARM

In the spring of 1971, the couple purchased a home in Westport, Connecticut. The new home, much like the home they called Middlefield, was an old farmhouse, this time an 1805 vintage federal farmhouse that also needed extensive renovation. Martha named the new home Turkey Hill Farm. To purchase the property, the couple exhausted every available means of financing available to them. As a result, they once again embarked on a stressful and exhausting renovation using their own hands and time because they couldn't afford to hire the labor of others. Both Martha and Andy always considered themselves diehard city people, yet the purchase and subsequent move to Turkey Hill Farm were lifestyle choices and an investment in the future. The move was also precipitated by Bangor Punta Corporation's move to Greenwich, Connecticut, 30 miles north of New York. Although the move afforded Andy a much easier commute, Martha continued to commute daily into New York City.

Once again, Martha and Andy completed most of the work themselves and eventually the home became a showplace. In her book *Martha Stewart's Gardening,* published in 1991, Martha writes about Turkey Hill Farm: "My husband, five-year-old daughter, and I had outgrown our New York City apartment and craved a place in the country...the proportions were lovely, but rented out for fifty years...it had fallen into great disrepair...we loved it from the very first. Here was the place where we could realize our dreams of a home, and a garden."[7]

While she continued as a stockbroker at Monness, Williams & Sidel, commuting into the city during the week, Martha focused on making Turkey Hill Farm into a beautiful home. Her brother, George, remembered it this way: "They never stopped working on that house. People would come over and they would never stop working while visitors were there. And the visitors would feel like they had to pitch in. Some were uncomfortable doing that. There was always something to do; that was part of her image...Martha is a workaholic. It's part of my family's makeup—everybody works at something."[8]

Not long after Martha, Andy, and Lexi moved from the city to Westport, the hectic schedule and hard work began to take a toll. Although the purpose of their move to Westport was to live away from the city and to live the life that Martha had dreamed of since she was a girl, the change, along with continuing pressures in her life as a stockbroker, brought to the surface many problems that had been developing. Martha and Andy's 11-year marriage steadily weakened as a result of the pace, pressures, and hard work. As well, Lexi hadn't easily weathered the changes in her home and school.

While living in the city, Lexi attended a private school and was with her parents in the evenings and on the weekends. In Westport, she was enrolled as a first grader at a local elementary school. As a result of the all the changes at home and at school, Lexi had difficulty making new friends; to her parents and family friends, she seemed very unhappy. With the constant work surrounding the renovation of their home, and with her parents' hectic work schedules and pressures, Lexi turned inward. The decision was made to make her bedroom the first room that was remodeled so that she had a place to go to escape the disarray of the rest of the house. Also, Martha and Andy enrolled her in a private school, where she seemed to do better. All the while, the Stewarts spent all their free time turning Turkey Hill Farm into the show place it would eventually become. Through it all, Martha began to take out her frustrations of the renovation, of Lexi's problems in school and at home, and the stress and difficulties she was experiencing as a stockbroker, on Andy.

By this time, there was a boom on Wall Street, and Martha's commissions from the stocks that the firm was promoting evidenced her ability to sell, her ability to convince clients to buy, and her drive to succeed. Many of her clients were institutions, but she also sold securities to individuals and had convinced many of her friends to purchase various stocks, including that of the furniture giant, Levitz Furniture. Monness, Williams & Sidel, and Martha individually were highly touting Levitz stock at the time. Just as there had been a boom in the stock market, however, a downturn in the economy and the political issues surrounding the Watergate scandal had an impact on the stock market. As a result, the furniture giant, who had seen rapid growth in the prior years, was left with large inventories. When the company announced disappointing earnings, the stock value fell, and many brokerage clients saw their holdings and their portfolio devalued. Martha felt embarrassed by the situation surrounding Levitz Furniture and that she, the firm, and her colleagues had highly recommended the stock to investors. With an unstable stock market; the embarrassment she felt after selling the Levitz Furniture stock to her clients, many of whom had lost money on their investment; and the fact that her schedule, work load, and the stress of Wall Street was affecting her marriage, in 1973, Martha decided to resign from Monness, Williams & Sidel.

A NEW CAREER—THE UNCATERED AFFAIR

For perhaps the first time, Martha was without a career and an identity. The resignation from the brokerage firm left her feeling dispirited and concerned about her next venture. She wondered how she could reconstruct a career or begin yet another one. Throwing herself into painting, gardening, and the renovation of Turkey Hill Farm, Martha considered what to do next. For a time, she considered selling real estate. It seemed a likely career path, as she knew houses and had a vision of what homes could become. She was a salesman, clearly evidenced by her success as a stockbroker. She took the test and earned her real estate license. Real estate and her love of architecture, landscaping, and decorating seemed a natural fit. She soon realized, however, that the actual work of selling houses involved spending many hours driving around with clients, something she didn't really want to do. She left the business without ever hosting an open house or selling a single property.

Still unsure of what she should do next, Martha continued with the renovation and was, for the first time, a full-time wife and mother. She was on ladders, in the garden, constantly starting and completing projects around the house. She stenciled floors, painted walls, carefully ironed bed sheets, and meticulously mowed the lawns. Still, she was clearly unhappy and unsure of what to do next. The solution came from a friend, colleague, and past mentor. Norma Collier, the woman who was assigned to be her chaperone when Martha was selected as *Glamour* magazine's "Best Dressed College Girl of 1961," presented the idea of opening a catering business. Collier said that she and Martha became very good friends right away. Martha was her children's godmother and she was Alexis's godmother. Norma said that they were very close, like a family, spending the holidays together and that they even had keys to each other's houses.[9]

Martha was quickly drawn to the idea of opening a catering business from her basement at Turkey Hill Farm. She and Norma, who had retired from modeling and was also looking for a new career while living in New Canaan, Connecticut, not far from Turkey Hill, hatched an idea. They became 50/50 partners in a new venture called The Uncatered Affair. They offered a service that no other catering business in the area offered—providing catered food in such as way that it appeared the client had prepared it. On the day before an event, The Uncatered Affair picked up the necessary kitchen utensils and cookware from the client's own home. When the food was delivered to the client, the food was presented using the client's own dishes and utensils. Catering staff was also provided to serve the food, set up the dining area, and provide decorations to fit the event.

Martha and Norma developed the new business from their respective hometowns, and the profits were split equally. Martha had seemingly found her calling, reminiscent of her days of giving parties where she enjoyed planning, cooking, entertaining guests, and reveled in the presentation of it all. Martha wrote about her early catering career in her book *Entertaining,* stating that her catering business began by chance and that as her experience with food and entertaining grew, she contributed articles to magazines and became a food editor. She wrote: "Suddenly food had a new national importance. Fashion magazines created lavish food and entertaining departments; all newspapers hired restaurant critics, who became public figures. Men began to cook. And each year hundreds of cookbooks appeared, extolling undiscovered and rediscovered cuisines, reminding us of the epicurean philosopher Brillat-Savarin's aphorism, 'Tell me what you eatest and I will tell you what thou art.' "[10] For Martha, what began by chance soon blossomed into a profitable business.

As Martha was busy growing the catering business, a new career unfolded for Andy. In 1973, at the age of 35, he left his position of assistant in-house legal counsel at Bangor Punta, a multinational mining conglomerate, for the more glamorous, faster paced world of publishing. His boss at Bangor Punta had been hired by Times Mirror Company's magazine and book publishing operations as the head legal counsel. Andy saw an opportunity for himself and moved to Times Mirror, becoming the second in command of the legal department. The new job had prestige and a higher salary, which made Martha very happy. She also saw his new job as an opportunity, for she had long dreamed of publishing a cookbook and thought Andy's position and publishing expertise would be more than helpful in this endeavor. After all, at the time, Times Mirror was a media giant, owning numerous magazines, newspapers, and book affiliates. Fortuitously, as a result of the quick departure of one of the division heads at Times Mirror, Andy became the new president and chief executive officer of Abrams Publishing, one of the book imprints at Times Mirror. He quickly immersed himself in all aspects of the publishing industry including the economics, production, marketing, and delivery systems.

Early in 1975, about six months after The Uncatered Affair opened for business, Martha and Norma dissolved their partnership. In his book *Martha Inc.*, Christopher Byron describes the reasons surrounding the split:

> The collapse came about because Martha, realizing she had a winner on her hands, began increasingly to push Norma aside. She did it with the same needling, belittling asides that Eddie Kostyra (Martha's father) had used to claim territory in his struggle to dominate Martha Sr.—the same approach that Martha Jr. witnessed as a child, and by now was using to dominate and control Andy. The pattern was always the same: The more that the target of her abuse would retreat, the more she'd advance, and the more aggressive and hurtful would become her attacks."[11]

Byron quotes Norma Collier as stating: "We'd be holding a cooking class in my kitchen for women from the area and Martha would constantly interrupt what I'd be saying and announce that I wasn't doing something right or some put-down like that. And I'd just stand there dumbstruck at her rudeness, and the class would come to an end, and she'd sweep up her things and leave."[12]

According to Byron, the end came when Norma overheard a conversation between Martha and Andy in the kitchen at Turkey Hill, where the two women were preparing for a party. She realized that Martha had been arranging for catering jobs and taking the income without informing her. She said she was shocked and felt a fool. She remembered being hurt financially years before when Martha worked as a stockbroker and she had lost money in the Levitz Furniture stock trade. Now, Norma said, she was being ripped off all over again. Norma told Martha that she'd had enough and didn't intend to continue the partnership.[13]

In the mid-1970s, having separated from the partnership with Norma Collier, Martha continued to build the catering business on her own. She continuously looked for ways to expand the business and increase her exposure. One way she increased business and her reputation was by opening another new business. In the town of Westport, amid a collection of high-end retail shops, called The Common Market, was a small food court where every afternoon, customers could have high tea and shop for unique food items, some brought in from Great Britain, some from New York. Martha was interested in what was happening at The Common Market and she thought she could sell homemade pies and other bakery goods, along with freshly prepared dinner food to the shop's clientele.

Persuading a shop owner to allow her sell her bakery and dinner items at a table by the entrance, she opened a new business she called The Market Basket. As the business grew, Martha gave up the table and opened a stand-alone store. She also continued with the catering business on her own out of her home. The Market Basket quickly became a success.

Realizing what she had built and enjoying the success and her subsequent notoriety in Westport and the surrounding area, in January 1977, Martha incorporated herself, naming the new enterprise Martha Stewart Inc. The new business, formed with high expectations to expand, was initially based out of her home at Turkey Hill Farm. It was just the beginning of the meteoric rise of Martha Stewart.

NOTES

1. Martha Stewart, *Martha Stewart's Quick Cook* (New York: Clarkson N. Potter, 1983), 116.

2. Jerry Oppenheimer, *Just Desserts* (Boca Raton: American Media, 2003), 129.

3. Ibid., 135.

4. Ibid., 145.

5. Stewart, *Martha Stewart's Quick Cook*, 9.

6. Ibid., 207.

7. Martha Stewart, *Martha Stewart's Gardening* (New York: Clarkson N. Potter, 1991), 9.

8. Lloyd Allen, *Being Martha* (New Jersey: John Wiley & Sons, 2006), 66.

9. Oppenheimer, *Just Desserts*, 90–91.

10. Martha Stewart, *Entertaining* (New York: Clarkson N. Potter, 1982), 6.

11. Christopher Byron, *Martha Inc.* (New York: John Wiley & Sons, 2003), 93.

12. Ibid.

13. Ibid., 93–94.

Chapter 5

IN THE PUBLIC EYE, MARTHA STEWART INC., AND THE FIRST BOOK, *ENTERTAINING*

I think she is hugely important for vast numbers of American women who are growing up without learning how to cook at their mother's knee. Martha's appeal is not just to career or middle-class women, but to the aspirations and social mobility of a lot of women who want to learn about everything that goes with the food, about table settings and design.

—Hillary Clinton

My ideas are good. I know what women want.

—Martha Stewart

Martha is, and always has been, a woman that never rests. Since she was a girl, she always believed that nothing was insurmountable and that taking each opportunity to the fullest was essential. In all of her life, she was never described as lazy or without ideas. Instead, she has been described as quick minded, aggressive, and since opening the catering business, she had added "smart businesswoman" to her resume. Expanding her business opportunities, constantly mindful of what else she could do, she was consumed with seizing each opportunity with passion, intending to enhance her personal exposure, and earning more money. To Martha, there is not, and never has been, another way to work except to work hard, maintain a strict schedule, and keep pace to meet deadlines. Martha's mantra long ago became "stay focused and work to the max!"

Before opening The Market Basket in Westport, Martha sold sumptuous desserts and dinner items from a table set up just inside the door of a small retail shop, one of several upscale shops collectively known as The Common Market. After dissolving the partnership with Norma Collier and The Uncatered Affair, she spent a great deal of time developing her own catering business. She was also always looking for new enterprises and ways to increase her visibility and earning power. Interested in the upscale specialty shops at The Common Market and the customers that shopped there, Martha had approached the owners about taking over the food section of the mall. As part of her pitch, she said she would give the retail area new interest by offering home-cooked food, noting that it would be similar to what she was known for at The Uncatered Affair.

Her pitch was timely as it coincided with what was happening in the workplace. By this time, more women were working outside of the home. Life for many of these working women was busier, frequently hectic, and, as a result, often more stressful. Many of them were raising a family and managing full-time careers at the same time. As a result, many of these women were looking for ways to make their own lives and that of their families easier, and certainly less stressful if at all possible. Convenience became a real issue and Martha knew it. She found a way to offer convenience, a good product, and the means to an easier working day for many of the working men and women in the Westport area. Martha knew that at the time, several stores in New York were offering freshly prepared food that could be picked up on the way home and enjoyed there. Many shoppers looked for food that was tasty and convenient but that was not a frozen dinner. The owners of The Common Market were well aware of this trend, too, and were impressed by Martha's proposal. To provide more of her proposal's details and to also present to the owners what she could do from her own kitchen, Martha set up a luncheon at Turkey Hill Farm. Gail Leichtman-Macht, co-owner and developer of The Common Market, said the luncheon was *all* Martha, the kitchen was warm and wonderful, and Martha prepared and served a fine herb omelet; but she also felt intimidated, despite Martha being very appealing and attractive. She said:

> At the same time—and I didn't believe her. She didn't feel *real* to me. I felt that she was almost *too* good to be true and that it was really important for her to present perfection as opposed to a vulnerable self or a natural self. There was a kind of practiced, skillful approach to doing things, and it went from the way she prepared the food, to the way she spoke, to the way she kind of engineered things. At that lunch I knew she had a plan that was *definitely* of her own making. She had it all in her head and

the wheels were always turning. She knew what she wanted to accomplish and how she wanted to accomplish it, and she pulled it off. She made a lovely lunch. And we hired her.[1]

Soon after the luncheon, Martha was offered a weekly salary, and after agreeing to share profits with catering jobs obtained through the store, Martha quickly opened The Market Basket. The success of this business was certainly the result of Martha's hard work and dedication to offering the best food products possible. The reputation of the shop and food quickly grew after word had spread that the woman who had catered so many of the parties in Westport and the surrounding area was offering the same delicious food at her store. Nearly overwhelmed with the demand and to satisfy her customers, Martha decided she needed to increase her output. To do that, she knew she needed help. The idea of subcontractors providing their best pies, cakes, cookies, and dinner dishes, their own home cooking, seemed to be the answer. To find the help she needed, Martha placed an ad in the *Westport News* for wonderful bakers or good cooks who wanted to be involved in a new and exciting food concept in Fairfield County.[2]

Soon her phone began to ring and before long, cooks and bakers from the Westport area offered their culinary skills, making their pies, cookies, and other dishes in their homes, and then delivering them to Martha to be sold by the Market Basket. Although the idea was a success, the local health department began to ask questions. Where were the desserts and dinner items cooked and under what conditions? How was the food transported? Food was being sold to the public; however, there was no license and no commercial kitchen space. Martha understood the concerns and quickly made the necessary changes to keep the business going. As the health inspectors were staked out in the parking lot, and as questions about the legality of the precooked foods sold in the Market Basket were being asked, a full working, licensed kitchen was installed.

With the health inspections and the legal questions about the Market Basket solved, other problems arose in the relationship between Martha and the owners of The Common Market. Word had spread that although much of the success of the Market was due to Martha's hard work, she was often absent from the premises. Questions were also being raised in regard to the agreement that Martha and the store owners would split the income earned from the catering jobs that were related to the store. The final straw came when a writer for *The New York Times* wrote a story about the Market Basket based on an interview with Martha. Describing herself as the proprietor, the co-owners were outraged that Martha gave the impression in the article that she owned The Market Basket. Gail Leichtman-Macht, co-owner and developer of The Common Market, related that Martha came to a meeting about the article armed with a dictionary that said proprietor was defined as "manager" and that she was, in fact, the manager of the Market Basket. Despite this rationalization and in combination with the other problems that had arisen about the Market Basket, Martha's relationship with The Common Market was terminated. Keeping this a secret from the employees, Martha related that she was leaving to concentrate her efforts on her own catering business.

After leaving the Market Basket, and after incorporating herself as Martha Stewart Inc., Martha was becoming more aggressive in her drive to succeed, determined to expand her business horizons, and increase her exposure in the community. She also concentrated on growing her earning potential.

Meanwhile, at Abrams Publishing, Andy was experiencing enormous success and was relishing his position in a more creative environment. It was apparent to friends and family that the Stewarts were enjoying great success in their careers. On the domestic front, however, nothing seemed right. Friends speculated that Martha's drive for success and perfection stemmed from unresolved issues with her father, Edward, and that Andy was often the target of many of those unresolved issues. Martha slowly began to tread on Andy, just like Edward had done to his family. Martha had seemingly shifted her resentments of her father to Andy.

In the midst of the tension and anger at home and in a deteriorating relationship, Andy struggled with the sudden news that he had cancer. This new threat to Andy and to the Stewarts came as a great shock. The diagnosis came after an accident that happened in the spring of 1977 when Andy and Martha's younger brother, George, went on a canoeing trip. George had often spent time with the Stewarts at their homes at Middlefield and Turkey Hill Farm, using his older sister's home as a sort of refuge from their father, Edward, and from other troubles that often seemed to surround him. Unlike his two older brothers, Eric and Frank, George never had the courage to fight back when his father unleashed his anger. After graduating from Rutgers and obtaining a position with Sears, George left his career at the retail giant and moved to Turkey Hill Farm where he became a carpenter's apprentice, a job that he felt was nearer to his calling. With Martha's help, he eventually opened a contracting business.

On the spring day in 1977, as Andy and George negotiated the river rapids in their canoe, the canoe overturned, and Andy slammed into a rock, bruising his hip. The injury healed and Andy nearly forgot about it until he later discovered a lump where the bruise had been. After seeing a doctor, he was quickly scheduled for surgical biopsy, which showed cancer. Cancer therapy was immediately recommended. Because the outcome after the treatments was uncertain, Andy was overcome with fear and chose to keep his illness a secret from his co-workers. As Andy endured the debilitating radiation treatments, friends noticed that Martha had gone into what some described as a terrible depression. One friend said that Martha had literally collapsed and that after Andy's surgery, he found Martha in a darkened room, feeling shattered and hopeless. Holding her hand while she cried, Martha said she was nothing without Andy, and that she was totally dependent on him; if she lost him, she wouldn't know what to do.[3]

Other friends said that at the time, Martha was taking a long and hard look into what the future held for her now that Andy's life was in jeopardy. One friend said that before Andy's cancer, they weren't a happy couple and when Andy got sick, it seemed they were close again. The illness, however, may have given Martha the incentive to push harder and faster, as she was thinking about her future. She wondered what would happen to the perfect world she was trying to create.[4]

Friends had for years noticed the apparent marital difficulties. They noticed, too, how Martha treated Andy with verbal abuse and harsh criticism. Now some were surprised at the compassion she showed her husband during his illness. Despite the history of Martha's controlling nature and her frequent temper tantrums directed at her husband, she was also possessive of Andy, especially as he was being treated for cancer. Despite their relationship problems, Andy hoped some good would come out of his illness. He hoped that Martha would soften toward him, that the tragedy would bring them closer together. Instead, Martha blamed Andy for going canoeing and getting hurt, and she blamed him for his cancer. When Andy finished his radiation treatments, he was told it would be five years before he could be sure the cancer was gone. After leaving The Market Basket and concentrating her efforts on the catering business, Martha's personal life seemed to be in a state of chaos, a state she wasn't used to and certainly did not like or want. The uncertainty of Andy's health contributed heavily to the anxiety between the couple and to their already enormously stressful lives.

At about the same time, Edward Kostyra's health began to fail. He was experiencing heart problems that had developed over the years and was treating himself for angina, only one of his many symptoms. He needed open-heart surgery, but he was treating his pain with alcohol.

Martha had been aware of her father's drinking problems and although he was someone she had always idolized, and despite the many unresolved issues she had with him, she was disappointed and concerned. Edward often visited her in Westport, and she finally convinced him to get the surgery he so desperately needed. He entered a hospital in New York City, but while resting to gain strength to withstand the difficult surgery, he died suddenly on August 31, 1979, just 10 days after his 68th birthday. He was buried in the family plot in Nutley, New Jersey. After the funeral service, Martha prepared a luncheon for family and friends at the family home at Elm Place before returning to Westport. She said that the most important and most influential man in her life was gone forever.

Despite the loss of her father and the continued difficulties in her personal life, Martha continued to work a frenetic pace, running faster than everyone else. She continued to operate on the edge, motivated by what she was accomplishing, knowing that hard work would keep her going. She was focused and kept her eye on everything around her. Knowing she needed little sleep or relaxation to survive, Martha built on her continued successes, looking forward to the next opportunity, enhancing her personal exposure, always building her business acumen, and always looking for ways to earn money and increase her business. She and her business, Martha Stewart Inc., thrived and flourished. Martha's brother George says that his sister is special like an artist is special and when you add in her great intellect, she is someone who doesn't behave like everyone else. When you think of ordinariness, he says, you shouldn't think of Martha because she isn't put together that way.[5]

MARTHA'S FIRST BOOK, *ENTERTAINING*

After his debilitating cancer treatment, Andy was back to work full-time and his career at Abrams Publishing was once again on an upward spiral. Martha continued to generate catering jobs, from small dinner parties to lavish events, with the number of guests ranging from about a dozen to several hundred. As the business grew and as she made important contacts, ideas continued to swirl in her mind. Since Andy's move into publishing, Martha had given a great deal of thought to publishing a cookbook. Until then, however, the idea of the book remained just that, an idea. At a launch party for one of the books published by Abrams, the idea took on more shape. Alan Mirken, the president of the Crown Publishing Group, attended the party and raved about the food. Asking Andy who the caterer was, he was introduced to Martha. This was Martha's first introduction to the soon-to-be publisher of her first book, *Entertaining*. Mirken remembered the introduction, stating he felt very lucky to be at the party. He described the party as extraordinary and that he was completely taken by what he experienced. Mirken told Martha she should think about writing a book, and Martha answered that she wasn't ready yet, but she hoped to be soon. Mirken thought he had just met a very talented person. The food, he said, was very good and very different, and the whole party was quite extraordinary and unique. Believing Martha had the potential to write a book, he felt fortunate to be in the right place to make the right suggestion.[6]

By this time in the late 1970s, as Martha's business flourished and she became more well known, there was a great interest in home cooking and the cookbook industry was growing. And although Martha had long considered the notion of publishing her own cookbook, she was well aware of the cookbooks that were being published every year. She saw herself as someone who could speak to anyone with an interest in cooking and entertaining, not just the wealthy or the upscale market. She felt strongly that her advice, and the books she wanted to write and publish, would appeal to a wide market, not just the wealthy or the upscale reader. With this in mind, she thought it was an excellent time to publish a book like *Entertaining*. The prominent food writer and critic Richard Sax observed later that Martha published her book at the exact moment when the food world was bursting. He noted that it seemed that everyone was publishing a cookbook and that suddenly there were four food magazines instead of one or two. He observed that there were cooking classes and cooking tips, that a food revolution was happening, and that people were being exposed to new and different kinds of cooking. It was the beginning, he said, of a new age of food and Martha was in the right place at the right time with the right idea.[7]

With Andy's experience in the publishing business and Martha's creativity, Mirken was confident that she could produce a marketable manuscript. From the fortuitous meeting, at which Mirken was so impressed with the food and then with Martha herself, came a contract, negotiated by Andy on Martha's behalf. With the contract signed, she began to plan the book from her home base at Turkey Hill. Martha believed her new book should convey to the reader ideas of how to entertain, with good food and a certain style. She also believed the book should target a wide audience, not just the wealthy. She and Andy agreed that the book should have many photographs, most of which would be taken from the parties and events Martha had catered. The intent was to have sumptuous pictures of food, with Martha showcased in the preparation and the presentation.

This, she knew, would convey to the reader a certain lifestyle. In fact, the book became an elaborate guide to being a good host.

While Andy took on the task of photo editing and page layout, the question of writing the book became an issue. Andy thought that a professional writer should write the book. Martha agreed. She had her catering business to manage and business was booming. Elizabeth Hawes, a former editor for *The New Yorker* and the spouse of Davis Weinstock, one of several individuals who had years earlier guided Martha to the brokerage business, came on board to interview Martha and write the book. It was important to Martha that she work with a writer she knew and thought she could control. After all, it was her name on the book, and she was showcased on nearly every page. And while she thought she couldn't write the book herself, she wanted it to be perfect. While planning the book she intended to title *Entertaining*, the catering business flourished and the work doubled in intensity.

According to Martha's brother George, the book took three years to produce and every plate was photographed by a professional photographer or by Andy, who attended the events with his camera in hand. With competitions for the best vegetable platters, everyone working for Martha went to great lengths to win. Martha set high standards and everything had to be perfectly designed.

George noted:

> While it was excruciatingly hard work, it was fun. These people would come to work for Martha, come in on fire and then go whizzing off and burnt out with nothing to show for it except recognition in this book or that book. They'd claim she was stealing ideas and doing this and that, but they were fully aware of what was happening. [Martha's] creativity is just phenomenal and she feeds everyone's creativity. That's not to say she hasn't hired talented people. She has, but she knows how to get them to create more than they ever thought they had in themselves.[8]

Martha knew that writing a cookbook wasn't enough. She also knew that a book that was *just a cookbook* wasn't enough either. She knew there was wide audience of readers who wanted to know how to organize for a party, set the perfect table, how to furnish a house, and how to plan a garden. And if they didn't want to do it themselves, they wanted to read about it—perhaps fantasize about it. *Entertaining*, published in 1982, was an elaborate guide to being a good host, and it was *just* the beginning of yet another part of Martha's business empire.

Entertaining was published to excellent reviews. The format was known as "coffee table" size, and it was the first book of its kind to be in full color. By 1985, Martha published four more cooking and entertaining books, continued to operate her catering business, and ran entertaining seminars where attendees from all over the country paid as much as $900 per person for tuition and lunch. By 1998, *Entertaining* was in its 30th printing. In her *Newsweek* article, Laura Shapiro described Martha as "the Barbara Cartland (well-known British romance author) of food, and she has a succinct explanation for her phenomenal success—"My ideas are good," she (Martha) states. "I know what women want."[9]

About the success of *Entertaining*, Martha said:

> To me, the success of my first book *Entertaining* says that people are paying attention to details and are confident about expressing themselves in their own way. . .pride in these details reflects an affection for the simple rhythms of life, which are not trivial at all. So many people have forgotten but are rediscovering the satisfaction of planting a garden, decorating a house, planning a wedding, and finding them important forms of expression.[10]

Martha's quick domination over a crowded field of books published every year and the dozens of food experts who clamor for attention in print and on TV has little to do with good eating. Filled with sumptuous photos, her books showcase Martha herself starring in what she calls "the lifestyle." "Without those pictures, the books would be useful but not fabulous," she said.[11] Her legions of fans readily agree.

NOTES

1. Jerry Oppenheimer, *Just Desserts* (Boca Raton: American Media, 2003), 190.
2. Lloyd Allen, *Being Martha* (Hoboken, N.J.: John Wiley & Sons, 2006), 75.
3. Jerry Oppenheimer, *Just Desserts* (Boca Raton: American Media, 2003), 200.
4. Ibid.
5. Allen, *Being Martha*, 113.
6. Oppenheimer, *Just Desserts*, 231.
7. Ibid., 235.
8. Allen, *Being Martha*, 111.
9. Laura Shapiro, "The Art of Showing Off," *Newsweek*, 1 December 1986, 66.
10. Martha Stewart, *Martha Stewart's Weddings* (New York: Clarkson N. Potter, 1987), 14.
11. Shapiro, "The Art of Showing Off," 66.

Martha Stewart's early business ventures included a home-based catering business; she has now become a cultural icon. Courtesy of Photofest.

Martha gained fame through publications about entertaining, decorating, and gardening. Courtesy of Photofest.

In 1997, Martha moves
from the Today show on
NBC to CBS's This Morn-
ing. Courtesy of Photofest.
© 1997, CBS Inc.

Following her March 4,
2005, release from Alderson
Prison after serving a federal
prison term, Martha walks
to a private jet. Courtesy of
Corbis. © LARRY DOWN-
ING/Reuters.

As part of a carefully planned comeback, Martha starred in her own version of the television show The Apprentice. She is pictured here with Donald Trump. Courtesy of Photofest. © NBC Photographer: Virginia Sherwood; Writer-Editor: ESB.

Martha's daughter Alexis—shown here with her mother and the Martha Stewart Living Omnimedia chairman of the board, Charles Koppelman—was a consultant for The Apprentice. Courtesy of Photofest. © NBC; Writer-Editor: ESB.

Chapter 6

KMART, TELEVISION, DIVORCE, OMNIMEDIA, GOING PUBLIC

I've always considered myself the ideal customer, the perfect example of the curious homemaker who needs help. I started brand Martha when I wrote my first book [Entertaining], to fill a void—entertaining. I started a magazine [Martha Stewart Living] to fill a void—entertaining. I started a TV show. I wanted to be comprehensive, expansive, all encompassing. I wanted to take a subject, not a brand. I took the subject of living. Martha Stewart just happens to be the name of the brand "Living." Other people are now picking up [that] name. I don't even own Living.com.
               —Martha Stewart

In 1977, when Martha incorporated her catering business as Martha Stewart Inc., she transformed it into more than just providing food for parties and events. What initially were small, intimate parties for friends and business associates became lavish celebrations for more than a thousand partygoers. Many of the events were "themed," creative, fun, and, to the partygoers, delicious and memorable. Martha provided everything for the event, from all the appropriate decorations, to lively entertainment that always complemented the theme, to all of the food befitting the designated idea sometimes put forth by Martha herself. By the beginning of the 1980s, Martha Stewart Inc. was catering affairs for celebrities, such as Paul Newman and Joanne Woodward, and for businesses such as Tiffany's, the famous jewelry store in New York City, and for Sotheby's, the renowned auction house. Along with her best-selling, widely popular book, *Entertaining*, Martha's reputation and fame grew. There is no doubt that by this time, Martha Stewart had arrived. She knew it, her clients knew it, and she was on her way to the fame and fortunate she had always dreamed of.

The foundation for *Entertaining*, published in 1982, was a how-to manual for entertaining in the home, from elaborate recipes, to a how-to for folding napkins, and what flowers were appropriate for the theme of the event. The initial press run of 25,000 copies was a gamble for the publisher, as it was for the time a greater number than was average for cookbooks. The book initially sold for $35.00, a cover price considered expensive for a cookbook and more than the average price for other cookbooks being published. The publisher was concerned that the new book that covered more than just cooking wouldn't sell well based on a higher than average cover price and would be considered too expensive by the average book buyer. For her part, Martha was discouraged by the number of books initially printed; she believed the publisher should have printed 35,000 to 40,000 copies. In the end, Martha was correct. The demand was bigger than anticipated and book buyers eagerly bought the lavish book. *Entertaining* was considered a publishing phenomenon, despite rumors and actual claims of plagiarism by other cookbook authors and chefs.

With clients that included the rich and famous, and with a wildly successful first book on the shelves, Martha was on her way to becoming a domestic advising wonder. She was in demand, and her fame was on the rise. Despite some criticism of the book, it was enormously successful, and Martha quickly planned her next books. She authored *Martha Stewart's Quick Cook*, in 1983, and *Martha Stewart's Hors d'Oeuvres* in 1984. A fourth title, *Martha Stewart's Pies and Tarts*, was published in 1985, and the very popular *Weddings* was published in 1987.

As she wrote books, catered events, and traveled throughout the country promoting herself and her books, she continued to remodel the Turkey Hill property, determined to make it the showpiece she always envisioned it would be. As busy as she was, and with her fame continuing to grow, Martha had less time to devote to her personal life. Her upbringing and what she learned from her father, Edward, came into play constantly. From him, she had learned how to take control and how keep it, and how to run everything and everyone. This included her husband Andy and their daughter, Lexi. She was known to manage it all with army-like efficiency.

On the outside, Martha and Andy tried to portray a couple in love. They entertained and traveled; however, all the while their relationship was crumbling and Andy was outwardly unhappy. Lexi was a sullen teen. Martha appeared to be interested only in becoming more powerful, famous, and wealthy and had less and less time for her family. She was writing, lecturing, and paying attention to the catering business, all to further her own career. Nearly overnight, she had become a lifestyle expert, and she wanted more. What came next was her profitable, if sometimes shaky, relationship with the retail giant, Kmart.

THE RELATIONSHIP WITH KMART

In 1986, Joe Antonini was appointed president of the Kmart Corporation. Two years earlier, as an executive with Kmart, he attended a speech given by Barbara Loren-Snyder, a well-known marketing expert. A short time later, he arranged to meet with her to discuss the future of Kmart, hoping to use her marketing expertise. Known for not mincing her words, and giving advice that often wasn't what her clients wanted to hear, she gave Antonini her thoughts about the corporation and its merchandising. Antonini always remembered their conversation and on his appointment as president, he contacted Loren-Snyder again to speak with her about Kmart and how the company could revitalize sales and its image. He asked her to join a committee he was forming to evaluate every department within the store. She agreed to offer her expertise and, along with the other members of the new committee, she visited Kmart stores. One of her ideas that came out of her many store visits was to hire a spokesperson for the house wares division to promote the store's merchandise to a wider audience. In an effort to find just the right spokesperson, she visited bookstores where she kept seeing Martha's books. Believing they were appealing and that the author's looks were captivating, Loren-Snyder said in her presentation to the committee that while she was not a cook and had never heard of Martha Stewart, she thought that maybe she had found the woman they were looking for. Martha, she said, knew how to put together not only food but also things like centerpieces, and that Martha might be able to develop a line of linens and dinnerware. She described Martha to the committee as an attractive woman at the right age, a wife, and a mother, and that she believed Martha represented "America" to the consumer.[1]

While Loren-Snyder thought that Martha wasn't someone likely to shop at a Kmart store, she did believe Martha was someone the typical female Kmart shopper would aspire to be like. According to Christopher Byron, author of *Martha Inc.*, Loren-Snyder thought Martha had the style, grace, and good looks that would be perfect for the job.[2] She knew Martha

was everything the average Kmart shopper was not. While looking further into hiring Martha as a Kmart spokesperson, she contacted newspapers around the country, asking lifestyle editors and reporters if they
knew about Martha Stewart. Only 1 of the 10 she contacted had ever
heard of her. Surprised to find Martha's phone number listed in the phone
book, Loren-Snyder called Martha at Turkey Hill and said, "Martha, you
do not know me. You have no reason to know me. But I can make you a
multimillionaire and a star and it won't cost you a penny."[3] After an initial telephone conversation, Loren-Snyder sent a letter reiterating their
discussion. In anticipation of meeting with Martha, Loren-Snyder made
a proposal to the Kmart committee stating that Martha Stewart, lifestyle
expert and best-selling author, should be the new spokesperson for Kmart.
As part of her proposal, she provided Martha's books, her magazine, and
newspaper articles for the committee members to view. The committee
gave the go-ahead to offer Martha the position. Little did anyone know
that the deal would eventually make Martha one of the wealthiest and
best-known women in the world.

As Loren-Snyder was finalizing the proposal to present to Martha,
Martha and Andy's relationship had reached the breaking point. By February 1987, members of Martha's family, including her mother, sister,
and brother, were living close by. Lexi, a senior at Barnard College, was
dating Sam Waksal, a man nearly 20 years her senior and someone who
would later have an enormous impact on Martha's life. As various members of her family were always nearby, and as her relationship with Andy
was crumbling, Martha answered the phone call from Loren-Snyder and
began considering a new business venture, although she wasn't aware at
the time that the venture was with Kmart.

The proposal that Loren-Snyder presented included Martha as the
centerpiece of the advertising campaign for the corporation's home and
kitchen department. Her books would be sold at Kmart, and the stores
would also sell a product line bearing the Martha Stewart name. Adver-
tisements on television and in newspapers and magazines, all touting the
products, were also planned. The meeting to discuss the arrangement
was held at Andy's office. Loren-Snyder said that when she got to the
end of the discussion, she told Martha that the company she represented
was willing to offer a substantial fixed annual salary, plus expenses to
cover Martha's appearance at stores throughout the country. When she
told Martha that the company she represented was Kmart, she said Martha sighed and appeared disappointed. When she added that there were
2,300 Kmart stores in the country and that the Martha Stewart product line would appear in every store, Martha appeared to have softened

to the idea and that the potential dollars had changed Martha's mood. Then, Loren-Snyder said, Martha and Andy were both as high as they could be.[4]

On July 6, 1987, Martha signed the contract and asked that the press release announcing the contract sound as if she would be paid millions of dollars for her services. She didn't want the contract amount of $200,000 that was negotiated for five years as a Kmart "consultant" mentioned, as it seemed to Martha to be "too chintzy and small." Martha was more interested in the public knowing the total amount of what Kmart would be paying her.[5] The agreement between Martha and Kmart made headlines. At the party to announce the arrangement, one reporter for *The New York Times* wrote:

> Many strange combinations have come out of American kitchens in the 80s, but Kmart may have served up the pièce de résistance with its recent announcement that entertainment guru Martha Stewart has signed a five-year contract to be its national spokeswoman and a consultant for home fashions. For many who are familiar with Mrs. Stewart's brand of stylish party giving, conveyed in five lavishly illustrated books, the link with the nation's largest discount retailer might have seemed an odd combination—but then, people once laughed at goat cheese pizza, too."[6]

Although Martha's job didn't require her to be involved in product design, she was expected to be the spokesperson and consultant. But Martha wanted to be more involved. She wanted input and decision-making authority on any product that was associated with her name, and she made demands about how many of the products were manufactured. Many of her ideas were rejected, not because they weren't good ideas, but because they weren't right for Kmart customers. Martha's consulting arrangement with Kmart included designing, creating, evaluating, and overseeing a line of bedding and bath products, as well as making personal appearances for the corporation. Kmart would then give her a royalty on each branded item sold, using Martha's name, image, and reputation in advertising the products.[7]

MOVING TO TELEVISION

In his book *Just Desserts*, Jerry Oppenheimer states that according to one of his sources, Martha said from the beginning that she always wanted to be on television.[8] With her successful catering business and her best-selling books, along with her newly formed association with Kmart, Martha was determined to enter the world of television to expand her expertise and fame. After the huge success of *Entertaining* and the books that followed, and with the continued success of the catering business, Martha was becoming better known and her exposure was growing. Willard Scott, of the NBC News morning show, *Today*, visited Martha at Turkey Hill a few times, showing her gardens, fixing a Thanksgiving turkey, and having coffee with Andy in a polished kitchen. Although this exposure was important to Martha, she wanted her own show. It was through a generous introduction from Norma Collier, her former partner at The Uncatered Affair, that Martha was introduced to Peter Murray.

At the time, Murray was president of a production arm of a public television station in Washington, D.C. According to Jerry Oppenheimer, in his book *Just Desserts*, Murray thought he'd found in Martha the answer to his quest to find original programming that was similar to what was being produced at television stations in Boston and New York. He said that when her book *Entertaining* came out, he felt Martha was a natural for television. There was momentum, he said, and the country's interest in Martha Stewart had come alive, and the production values in *Entertaining* were enormous. Murray felt that Martha and Andy Stewart knew what they were doing in terms of product, but that the product wasn't only entertaining; it was Martha Stewart herself. This, he said, was what Martha had in mind from the beginning, that she was extremely focused, driven, and a hardworking person who was single-minded about her own success. He knew, just as Martha did, for whom she had created the book *Entertaining* and that she saw herself as a personality, and that it was getting on television that drove her all along. He added that Martha didn't see herself simply as a caterer, but as so much more.[9]

With Andy acting as her agent, and with Martha in control of the negotiations, a deal was signed for a lifestyle program. Soon, a pilot was filmed and a sponsor was found. Not long after, however, Murray resigned and another executive took over the project. After six months, the show never got off the ground. Undeterred that the show never aired, and taking the experience and the exposure it offered, Martha remained adamant about being on television. Then in 1986, in conjunction with WGBH-TV in Boston, with a mail-order video that followed, Martha's first television show, *Holiday Entertaining with Martha Stewart*, aired. The show was filmed six months before the airdate at Thanksgiving.

With her drive to complete more projects and to increase her business ventures, Martha's plate was full, but her personal life continued to spiral downward. Her fans saw a TV show where everything looked perfect, but little was perfect at Turkey Hill. Andy and Lexi refused to be a part of the production that showcased Martha and members of her family. And while the show was a complete success, with good reviews across the country, the production of the show highlighted what was going wrong at home. While a deal was made for more shows, and despite her full schedule and personal difficulties, Martha announced she had plans for a daily half-hour program. Scoffing at some criticism that the show didn't portray what was reality in American homes, Martha viewed the comments and the criticism as more publicity, and she declared that she was "about to conquer the world" and that her objective was to get as many people as she could, including viewers and book buyers, to want to improve their lives. She knew that people wanted to make things nicer for themselves, and that they wanted to look at a dish and say that it was great and remember to use it again. When asked if she found it incredible that she had become an authority on taste, she declared that she wasn't at all surprised and added that someone had to do it.[10]

MARTHA AND ANDY STEWART'S DIVORCE

In 1986, while Martha was working on the Thanksgiving special, she was also making the preparations for the next book *Weddings*, to be published in 1987. By the fall of that year, Andy suggested that he and Martha get marriage counseling, stating if the sessions didn't help, he would leave the marriage. In early 1987, he decided he'd had enough and secretly began to look for a place of his own. After revealing this to Martha, and admitting to not being faithful in the marriage, Martha asked Andy to stay in the marriage. The highly anticipated book *Weddings* was soon to be published and Martha knew a separation, or a scandal, wouldn't look good. When her book *Weddings* was published on April 1, 1987, the dedication was to Andy and their wedding, which, she said, would remain her favorite ceremony, and to her daughter Alexis, whose wedding she looked forward to with pleasure. The book also included several photographs of Andy and Martha on their July 1, 1961 wedding day.

Weddings, like most of her other books, was well received by the critics. In a review of the heavy tome, *The New York Times* described it was an ode to perfection, and at five pounds, it was luxuriously photographed, and a romantically written book. The *Times* quoted Martha as calling her latest work a social document of life in the 1980s, with brides depicted as icons. The *Times* also noted that the book featured Martha herself, and that she said she was committed to a certain kind of lifestyle.[11]

On the very day the article appeared in *The New York Times*, Andy was packing his bags, ready to end the marriage. Martha, meanwhile, stated to the *Times* and its readers, that she was already at work on her sixth and seventh book and that she had purchased another property near Turkey Hill. She added that she planned to write extensively about the renovation and also make a video of the complete restoration of the vintage property. Declaring that her books would always be first in her many projects, Martha said that she always tries to write about subjects nobody has treated in such a personal way and that what she was writing about is a lifestyle and a catalog of material that she has paid attention to for a long time. She added that she wants her books to be a standard of perfection from which people can pull ideas.[12]

The media and her many fans and readers did not know that Martha's marriage was in trouble. After all, the publisher hoped, as did Martha, that this book would position her as *the* wedding expert. She had her first booking on the *Oprah* show, and a lavish party to launch the book was planned. Martha met with Alan Mirken, her publisher at Crown Publishing Group, to advise him of the pending divorce. In the meeting, Mirken noted that the divorce was very troubling because Martha and Andy had been so close, and that it was a very difficult thing for Martha to come to grips with because she had always done everything she wanted to do. He thought she wanted at that point to stay married, and that Andy was likely a little bit lonely because Martha was so dedicated to her career.[13]

In April 1987, after nearly 27 years of marriage, Andy left Turkey Hill for good. Andy later told a friend that he had left Martha because she had gradually become a very difficult person. He described her as being selfish and that she was not truthful, was unpleasant, and was often rude and angry.[14] On April 24, 1987, the *New York Daily News* reported that Andy Stewart, whose wife Martha Stewart wrote the lavish coffee table book, *Weddings*, had been apartment hunting in New York and that their marriage had hit rocky waters. The newspaper noted that Andy's move had come at an awkward time, as Martha, a wedding authority and a syndicated columnist, was on a national tour for her book. The announcement noted that both Andy and Martha denied there were any marital difficulties and that the news of a divorce was completely false. Martha, the newspaper noted, had said that she and Andy were happily married.[15]

In March 1988, Andy filed for divorce, requesting that the court grant a division of the property. What Andy envisioned would take six months to settle instead took several years. It was Martha's belief that, because Andy had moved out and wanted to dissolve the marriage, everything belonged to her. Continually avoiding being served with papers to begin the divorce proceedings, Martha finally accepted service of the divorce complaint and filed a motion of her own to put a seal on all hearings and records in the divorce case. According to Jerry Oppenheimer, in *Just Desserts*, the motion read that Martha, as the defendant, requested that as a Kmart spokesperson and food consultant, the records be closed. The motion noted that national media exposure of the records could be detrimental to her reputation and her occupation and also to those not involved in the divorce actions, such as Kmart.[16]

By the time Andy filed for divorce, he had fallen in love with Robyn Whitney Fairclough. Robyn had known Martha and Andy for years and was a friend of Lexi. The two were close in age, and she had often worked with Martha in the catering business. Eventually Robyn became a flower-arranging consultant and worked on other projects for Martha. Once Martha learned of Andy and Robyn's relationship, she accused Andy of adultery, believing their relationship had started years before. Andy denied this claim, but it and many other claims all made for a fierce battle between Martha and Andy that lasted two years. The court issued a final decree in the summer of 1990 that ended the Stewart's marriage. According to Jerry Oppenheimer, in the book *Just Desserts*, Martha kept Turkey Hill and its contents, which were appraised at $900,000, and cash and securities. She also retained a home in Connecticut that she had purchased for her mother and sister. Andy was awarded acreage in upstate New York and the Middlefield cottage. According to the settlement, Martha was to pay Andy $1.5 million for his share of Turkey Hill. Andy was forced to recommence a lawsuit to force Martha to comply with the terms of the settlement. She finally paid Andy nearly five years after their divorce was final.[17]

TIME WARNER INC. AND OMNIMEDIA

As Andy was building his life with Robyn, Martha was determined to keep building her fame and fortune. She began thinking about what other books she still wanted to write, and she decided to form her own publishing company, giving her complete control over style, design, and content. At this time, the consulting arrangement with Kmart, which included designing, creating, and overseeing the product line that would bear her name and would make her a household name, was secure. Taking a list of book ideas to Crown Publishing, they determined they weren't interested in changing their current arrangement. It was October 1987, the stock market had recently plunged to an all-time low, and no one really knew how long the downturn would last. Undeterred by the economy or by

Crown Publishing refusing her proposal, Martha took her idea of her own publishing operation to Time-Life Books, the publishing arm of Time Inc. Based on some internal movement of personnel, her ideas that were at first met positively, lost ground.

By this time, Martha had decided to look beyond just book publishing and had formulated the idea of a new magazine that would bear her name. She went to Conde Nast Publishing, who after first feeling positive about a new venture developed a prototype that would feature Martha on every cover. On further discussions and review of the project, and also based on the other magazines that they were already publishing, and fearing a new similar magazine would confuse the market and jeopardize the success of those publications, they provided her with the prototype they had produced and allowed her to promote it to someone else.

After taking the idea and prototype to the Rupert Murdoch publishing corporation, she went back to Time Inc. By this time, as a result of a merger, Time Inc. had become Time Warner Inc. A division of Time Warner Inc., Time Publishing Ventures, reviewed the magazine prototype and decided that Martha was a woman with high visibility potential. The idea of a new magazine, prominently featuring Martha and all her ideas, was considered viable or at least more than just an interesting prospect. But it was also a big risk. After all, rumors of Martha's highly contentious divorce permeated the publishing industry. As a result, her reputation and that of Time Warner could be at risk. As well, circulation numbers of the most popular women magazines at the time were down, and producing yet another magazine aimed at the same market was taking a chance. Martha knew all about circulation numbers and the fact that many magazines were going out of business, but she was undaunted, saying that some people thought she must be nuts to start a magazine at a time when magazines were closing, but that she thought it was a very good time to begin a new magazine venture, and that it was a challenge. Time Warner Inc. knew that the success of a new magazine depended on Martha's name and her identification in the marketplace. Martha declared that she needed to maintain a presence, and that her readers liked to see her wearing a work shirt and digging in the dirt.[18]

After a great deal of discussion and investigation, Time Warner Inc. decided to go forward. Martha signed a letter of agreement to produce two issues that would be tested in the market place. The new magazine, *Martha Stewart Living*, was clearly Martha's vision, and she intended to be in control, with her name and image on each cover and her thoughts, ideas, opinions, and lifestyle recommendations featured within its content. It would be completely devoted to Martha. She knew her strengths and that she would have complete control of the magazine's content, but she still needed help with writing, layout, design, and production.

In conjunction with Time Warner, Martha got the help she needed, and in November 1990, copies of the new magazine went on the news-stand. The cover image was of Martha and she was featured on nearly every page. To almost everyone's surprise, the response to the magazine was good, but this was no surprise to Martha. As always, Martha was confident. She knew what she could do, what her readers wanted, and what should come next.

The immense response to the initial magazine, from more subscription orders than expected, and from people who hadn't even seen the magazine, to selling more ad space than anyone ever expected, astounded executives at Time Warner, Inc. It could safely be said that the nation, perhaps the world, had gone Martha Stewart crazy; and at Time Warner, Inc., Martha was suddenly gold. Time Warner declared the magazine's test issues a success and in June 1991, a 10-year contract for publication of the magazine was signed. The contract also included the production of television programs, videos, and books. An advertising campaign began with NBC's *Today* show where Martha would appear on a regular basis with a six- to eight-minute segment. The initial appearances became an embarrassment for her and the show. On one segment, Martha provided incorrect advice and reviewers responded negatively. Despite initial problems, the segments were a hit and ratings points rose when she was on the show.[19] Once again, Martha wanted more. She hoped NBC would contract with her to do a half-hour program. The NBC network passed on the proposal, but a deal was cut for a weekly half-hour program that would air on the Lifetime network. The show aired around the country and within a few years, it was the most popular women's program on morning television. Her popularity soared. Her friends and family noted that her energy level was almost frightening. Her life was at a frenetic pace and, thanks to her ambitions, she was one of the most recognized faces in America.

By 1993, Martha was the editor of one of the most popular magazines in the country. She had a popular weekly television program, was the author of 10 books and 6 videos, and continued to be a spokesperson for Kmart. She was a phenomenon and was seemingly everywhere. But although she was also a conglomerate, her various affiliations were disorganized. She needed to structure all the various interests so that she could continue to plan, further her career, and increase her exposure and fame. She also wanted to organize and restructure so that she would eventually have complete control of her various business assets. She needed someone to help her and she turned to Sharon Patrick, a former partner of McKinsey & Company, a New York management-consulting firm and then president of her own firm, the Sharon Patrick Company. She also enlisted the assistance of Allen Grubman, known in New York as the lawyer for the rich and famous, and someone who had great success in negotiating contracts for many entertainers, such as Madonna, Michael Jackson, and Billy Joel. In an article that appeared in *Working Woman* magazine in June 1995, Martha said that bringing in someone like Allen was good because he hadn't been with her while she was growing up, and that he didn't consider her to be the same old Martha. From day one, she said, Allen knew that she was a star and looked at her from a higher standpoint. Martha described Allen as someone who could schmooze, and that when you saw him negotiate, you knew he was schmoozing, but that he was the best negotiator she had ever seen. Martha learned a lot about negotiating from Allen, and said he was wonderful at what he did, and what he did for her.[20]

Sharon and Allen quickly became two of Martha's closest associates and advisors. They counseled Martha on how to organize her business and how she might restructure her relationship with Time Warner and Kmart. Martha knew *Martha Stewart Living* magazine was a complete success, as was her TV show. Knowing she brought great success to the business association, she believed that earning only a base salary that she considered minimal at best, despite the many perks afforded her, was not enough. As Christopher Byron states in *Martha Inc.*, "*She* was the message, *she* was the subject matter, *she* was the brand, with the magazine, the TV show, with everything."[21]

Martha was determined to earn more, believed she deserved more, and wanted a new contract. With Allen's help, Martha negotiated a new contract with, to her at least, better terms. At the beginning of 1995, she signed a new agreement with Time Warner, Inc. Still, however, Martha wanted more power and much more control. She began to make even more demands on Time Warner that at first were perceived as unreasonable, maybe even outrageous by industry standards at the time. Along with more perks and a bigger clothing allowance, she wanted a percentage of the equity in Time Warner. But what she really wanted to do was make so many demands that she would eventually be let out of her contract, giving her in effect 100 percent of all the profits.

It was always Martha's plan to gain complete control over *Martha Stewart Living* and to incorporate all of her businesses—books, television, online enterprises, and merchandizing—beneath one corporate umbrella. She knew that she alone had created a phenomenon and had built a very successful business. Now she wanted to call all the shots herself.

In the spring of 1996, any media company with an involvement in the online world was considered a sure, safe bet. It was the dot.com boom, deals were being negotiated and fortunes were being made, and Martha was one of the hottest personalities on television and on the newsstand. Martha knew she had to break free and with Sharon Patrick's help, she began planning how this could be accomplished. Together, they devised a plan for buyout capital for an exit from Time Warner. In early 1997, the capital was obtained and Martha gained control from Time Warner. The terms of the deal weren't disclosed, however it was reported in *The New York Times* that she paid $85 million.[22]

The result of all her demands and the extensive negotiations was her new company known as Martha Stewart Living Omnimedia Inc., including *Martha Stewart Living* magazine, which was no longer controlled by Time Warner. Martha was the chairman and Sharon Patrick the chief operating officer. Martha Stewart Living Omnimedia Inc., a publicly traded information company, was unique in American media. On October 19, 1999, the company went public, with Martha owning about 70 percent of the stock. Serving orange juice and breakfast snacks to the floor traders of the New York Stock Exchange, Martha rang the opening bell with the company's banner displayed behind her. At the end of the first day of trading, the company stock nearly tripled in value and Martha had a personal net worth of more than $1 billion. There was no doubt to her or to anyone that she had made it. She was now the chairman of the corporation and was known as the richest self-made woman in America. From humble beginnings in a middle-class neighborhood in New Jersey, she had become one of the wealthiest people in America. Once again, she had positioned her career move at just the right time to ensure complete achievement. The stock market was soaring, with prices reaching new highs, and investors were benefiting from a bull market, making many individuals billionaires. With a TV show, radio show, MarthaStewart .com, Martha by Mail, and the elegant pages of *Martha Stewart Living* magazine, Martha Stewart was seemingly everywhere. All her products, designs, advice, and merchandise were cross-promoted. Readers, viewers, and listeners learned to wrap a package in the just the right way, or make the perfect dessert for a bridal shower. They could easily order any of the promoted products through the Web site, the magazine, or by mail. She was everywhere and women—and some men too—across America cheered her on.

By the late 1990s, Martha was now one of the best-known and wealthiest women in America. In 1997, she was named one of America's 25 most influential people by *Time* magazine. And although her private life was difficult, she reminded her assistants, "Remember, I'm not Martha Stewart the person anymore, I'm Martha Stewart the lifestyle."[23]

Martha had always been someone to watch, but now she was one of the most closely watched women in America. Everything she said, did, advised, or promoted was written about. Martha was seemingly at the top of the world.

NOTES

1. Jerry Oppenheimer, *Just Desserts* (Boca Raton: American Media, 2003), 304.
2. Christopher Byron, *Martha Inc.* (New York: John Wiley & Sons, 2003), 137.
3. Ibid., 138.
4. Oppenheimer, *Just Desserts,* 307.
5. Byron, *Martha Inc.,* 155–156.
6. Ibid., 156.
7. Ibid., 181.
8. Oppenheimer, *Just Desserts,* 288.
9. Ibid., 289.
10. Ibid., 299.
11. Ibid., 315.
12. Ibid., 316.
13. Ibid., 317.
14. Ibid., 318.
15. Ibid., 319.
16. Ibid., 327.
17. Ibid., 367.
18. Ibid., 395.
19. Ibid., 398.
20. Ibid., 409.
21. Byron, *Martha Inc.,* 248.
22. Ibid., 292, 293.
23. Ibid., 195.

Chapter 7

THE INVESTIGATION

I have learned that I really cannot be destroyed.
                                        —Martha Stewart

The ubiquitous Martha, the same girl from Nutley, New Jersey, who began her entrepreneurial career with a catering business out of her home, once stated: "Well, my motto is living is limitless...and because it's limitless my day will never end, my opportunities will never end."[1] And since beginning that successful business, she has continued to move at break-neck speed. She and Sharon Patrick had carefully planned the purchase of *Martha Stewart Living* magazine from Time Warner Inc. in 1997, giving Martha complete control of its editorial content. Together, they also planned the initial public offering of the stock in Martha Stewart Living Omnimedia, which made Martha, who owned 71 percent of the stock, one of the wealthiest self-made women in America and a true media mogul.

The structure of Omnimedia put Martha, the living brand, at its center, with all other business interests—cooking, crafts, home, weddings, gardening, and holidays—radiating from there. All of the spokes of this carefully planned and managed business wheel were completely intertwined across all media avenues, with Martha always at the center. She firmly believed in cross-promotion and the power of relating all business interests to each other. Everything that had her name on it was her design, with a clearly defined strategy and lots of ideas. She continuously focused on where she and her brand were going. She once stated that her marketplace was as big as everyone who has a house and this realization of her market never wavered.

In an interview in *Adweek* magazine, on February 14, 2000, Martha was asked how she prioritized ideas and all those perceived opportunities:

> To take extreme care with that brand, to do nothing that you will regret later, nothing. That is a serious consideration...I have turned down many lucrative endorsements offers. I've made conscious (decisions). I do not get on the TV and sponsor GE light bulbs, for example...The great brands that are thriving have been extremely cautious to not disappoint, they've been extremely cautious to satisfy the customer, they've been extremely attentive to that customer. They don't want to misinterpret...As soon as you tell people what they want, you have to listen. I give people what they want and need; I don't tell them what they want and need. It's a very big difference.[2]

It was no surprise to anyone that Martha was seemingly everywhere, running a successful multimedia corporation in accordance with her own personal vision on about four hours sleep a night. But could the brand outlive Martha herself? After all, she was the personification of the brand and this tended to worry her investors and some of her fans. She had majority control of the corporation. Perhaps there was too much emphasis on Martha as a living brand. There needed to be a line of succession in the company to ensure the brand carried on and the corporation remained successful if Martha was no longer an essential part and seemingly vital to its success. To Martha, these were nonissues.

In January 2000, in response to such concerns, she stated: "I have imbued this company with a tremendous amount of my spirit and my artistic philosophy. So much that emerges here and now is a combination of that and other people's creativity." She was, she added, "confident her business could live on without her, despite her closeness to the brand."[3] In December 2000, she reiterated, "There's now a corporate structure in place, we've addressed succession head on. We're well-represented by others editorially, in merchandising and distribution." She added that for shareholders and fans alike, "It's a good thing."[4]

But investors and the board of directions continued to ask the questions of how much was too much Martha. And although her fans were seemingly satisfied, her detractors often were not. Martha Stewart and Martha Stewart Living Omnimedia were everywhere. She was high profile, extremely wealthy, and although her fan base grew and her popularity soared, there were many who tired of her, her persona, and her seemingly constant success. Little did she or anyone know how a sale of 3,928 shares of stock in a biotech company would affect her, the well-known high priestess of domesticity. No one could have anticipated how the events that would take place shortly after the sale of these share would greatly affect her, her corporation, colleagues, friends, family, and her fans, who always seemed to support her.

DR. SAM WAKSAL

When Martha ran her catering business, she catered parties for the wealthy, for celebrities, big charities, and small affairs for friends and family. Her parties were well attended and her reputation was well known from the beginning. At one such party for a charity, Martha first met Dr. Sam Waksal, a New York immunologist, businessman, and investor. At the time, Alexis, Martha's daughter, was a student at Barnard College, and while there she was introduced to Sam. The two began dating, even though Sam was many years her senior. They often stayed at Martha's home and after the relationship fell apart, Martha and Sam remained friends. Since then, Martha and Sam have sometimes been linked romantically, sometimes appearing together at social functions, and they've also often been the subjects of gossip columns. Sam, like Martha, owned a home in the fashionable Long Island village of East Hampton, and the two traveled in the same social circles. Sam also invested in some of Alexis's business ventures, including her sports and fitness club in New York. Martha and Sam's social and business relationship, which began in the 1980s, became one of Martha's most important and perhaps most devastating relationships.

Sam Waksal, the elder of two sons of World War II Holocaust survivors, grew up in Dayton, Ohio. After graduating with a doctorate degree in immunology, he worked at Stanford University, the National Cancer Institute, Tufts Medical School, and Mount Sinai School of Medicine before founding a biotech firm, ImClone Systems, in 1985. By this time, Martha and Sam were often thought to be more than friends. Indeed, their relationship was also linked financially. Martha invested in ImClone Systems, as did many other well-known individuals, including Martha's good friend from Westport, Connecticut, Mariana Pasternak. Martha was seemingly impressed by Sam's ability to climb the social ladder coming from humble beginnings in Ohio, and by his ability to attract the wealthiest celebrities and business people from around the world, inviting them to his lavish parties and asking them to invest in his company.

Indeed, Martha was so impressed that she agreed to cover Sam's daughter's wedding in *Martha Stewart Living* magazine in the summer of 1998.

PETER BACANOVIC

Another individual who played an important role in Martha's future was Peter Bacanovic. At a weekend party at Turkey Hill, Martha met Peter when he was a senior at Columbia College. Peter was already acquainted with Alexis, then a student at Martha's alma mater, Barnard College, a sister school of Columbia. Peter was good looking, personable, and the son of a socially well-connected New York family. He made quite an impression on Martha, especially in light of his family connections and his good looks and personality. She deemed him an appropriate match for her daughter. Peter also made a good impression on Sam, who eventually hired him to work at ImClone Systems. Peter worked at ImClone from 1990 to 1992. After leaving ImClone, he moved on to Merrill Lynch, where he built a brokerage portfolio that included investments for Martha, Sam, and Mariana and Bart Pasternak. This association of individuals and their individual investments in the biotech firm founded by Sam Waskal would eventually be the impetus that dramatically changed Martha's life forever.

Martha was one of the closely watched women in America. What Martha said and did were constantly monitored, idolized, and often mimicked and mocked. By 2001, Martha surpassed Oprah Winfrey as the most written about woman in America, and, with the exception of Queen Elizabeth, the most written about woman in the world. At the same time, many of the CEOs of companies in America had fallen from favor. In the 1990s, CEOs, especially those of big corporations, were applauded, and their business acumen celebrated. But by 2001, all this had changed. The stock market went from a bull market, with great growth and businesses expanding, to a more bearish market, where investors were selling, rather than buying, in anticipation of falling prices and business failures. Some companies collapsed or at the very least shrunk in size, causing layoffs and certainly tightening of belts. Technology companies, in particular, which had grown at a record pace in the 1990s, where many billionaires were made, collapsed in the early days of 2000. Investors saw their holdings diminish and workers of many corporations saw their retirement funds shrink, or in many cases vanish altogether. It wasn't a good time in corporate America and Martha, like many CEO's, was enduring criticism and even blame. She was also a woman at the head of a high-profile corporation.

ENRON CORPORATION AND LINKS TO OMNIMEDIA AND IMCLONE

In the midst of the stock market collapse and allegations of Wall Street abuse, Congress took particular notice of what was happening, and investigations into money laundering and insider trading began. The Subcommittee on Oversight and Investigations of the House Energy & Commerce Committee began investigating companies that included Enron Corporation, which had been named just a few years before as a company with excellent quality management. By the end of 2001, Enron was bankrupt; their auditor, Arthur Andersen, the auditing firm for Martha Stewart Living Omnimedia Inc., faced felony fraud charges. The Enron scandal was so big and encompassing that no one during the initial investigations really knew what exactly happened or who was involved.

As the fallout continued, many in America wanted answers and they wanted to know who was to blame for all the ills in American business; some speculated that the problems were deep and convoluted, affecting the U.S. economy, stature in the world, and investors losing money. As Enron was being investigated, its links to other corporations were being examined. As the investigations continued, threads that were interwoven between Enron and other corporations were followed. There were apparent connections between Enron, Martha Stewart Living Omnimedia, and ImClone. All three companies shared the auditing firm, Arthur Andersen, and all three had boards of directors linked by common friendships and board members.[5] As investigators continued to examine Enron, however, these commonalities were considered coincidences; and Martha was not a target of any investigation until early in 2002, when they took an interest in ImClone and possible insider trading activities. Martha owned shares of ImClone stock and was a close friend of Sam Waskal, the founder of ImClone.

SAM WAKSAL AS CEO OF IMCLONE SYSTEMS

Dr. Sam Waksal was known for his lavish lifestyle. What his friends and family didn't know were the details and depth of his financial problems. In early December 2001, he expected the Federal Drug Administration (FDA) to approve the marketing of ImClone's anticancer drug, Erbitux. The stock value of ImClone reflected this expected important approval, and Sam was more than confident that, as a result, his financial woes would soon be over, so confident in fact, that he decided he would take a Christmas vacation, spending time away from the business details. At Merrill

Lynch, Peter Bacanovic, Martha and Sam's stockbroker, was also away for the holidays, enjoying himself in Florida, leaving the stock portfolio that included ImClone investments to his assistant, Doug Faneuil.

While Sam was enjoying his friends at a posh resort in the Caribbean, word reached him on Christmas day that the FDA did not intend to approve the anticancer drug for market. Flying back to New York the day after Christmas, Sam knew the value of his shares of ImClone stock would plunge, resulting in his own financial ruin. His family and friends also owned shares in his company and they too would incur financial losses. Despite rules against insider trading, he called family and friends, advising them to sell ImClone stock. He also contacted his broker, only instead of speaking with Peter, who was out of town, he put a directive to Doug Faneuil that all of his 79,797 shares, and those shares owned personally by his daughter, should be sold immediately.

By mid-morning, Doug contacted Peter in Florida, alerting him to the sale of ImClone shares. Peter then called Martha; however, she and her good friend Mariana Pasternak had already boarded a private jet bound for Mexico for a holiday vacation. Because she was in flight, Peter had to leave a message with Martha's assistant, Ann Armstrong. The message stated, "Peter Bracanovic thinks ImClone is going to start trading downward."[6] Peter called Doug, his assistant, and informed him that when Martha returned the call, he should tell her about the Waksal stock transaction.

When her jet landed in San Antonio, Texas to refuel, Martha called Ann Armstrong for her messages. Hearing about the call from Doug at Merrill Lynch, she returned the call and was told that the ImClone stock had reached a new low of $60 per share. He also told Martha that he was instructed by Peter to inform her that Sam was selling his shares. Being relatively new to the stock industry and as Peter Baconovic's assistant, he may not have realized he had just broken a rule at Merrill Lynch, that of relaying information about one client to another. When she heard the news of Sam's sale, she too directed Doug to sell her 3,928 shares of Im-Clone stock. She then called Sam to find out what was happening at ImClone. Rather than speaking with Sam, she left the following message with his secretary: "Something's going on with ImClone, and I want to know what it is."[7] Boarding the jet for takeoff to Mexico, she told Mariana that she had just sold her ImClone stock and that Sam was trying to sell his. Martha, once a stockbroker herself, could not know that this day would be one of the most important days of her life.

After instructing her broker at Merrill Lynch to sell her shares of stock as a result of the information relayed to her, was she guilty of insider trading or just being prudent in her investments? Martha was once a stockbroker and knew the rules of obtaining and using insider information. Was it improper behavior for her stockbroker, Peter Bacanovic and his assistant, Doug Faneuil, to relay such information to Martha? Once Martha arrived in Mexico, she spoke to her daughter Alexis, and their discussions included what was happening at ImClone and with their mutual friend, Sam Waksal. On December 28, 2001, a fax arrived at the ImClone office stating that the FDA would not approve ImClone's application for the anticancer drug, Erbitux. An announcement by ImClone was made after the close of the trading day.

In Mexico, Martha told her friend Mariana, "Isn't it nice to have brokers who tell you those things?"[8] Was it being nice or was it insider trading? She had directed her broker to sell her shares based on information she had received about the company. Had she and her broker discussed the sale of these shares before hearing about the FDA's decision? Why would Martha, who was worth so much, risk so much and sell her shares using this information?

These questions and many others like them were asked of Martha and Peter once the investigation into possible insider trading activities began in earnest. In response to Martha's role and any insider trading activities, she and Peter told investigators that they had had discussions about ImClone as part of a regular portfolio review in the fall of 2001. Martha had decided at the time to hold the shares, believing it would continue to increase in price and her investment would grow in value. According to Peter, he asked Martha about selling the stock, if not now, when? In his later testimony, he stated that he and Martha had come to a verbal agreement to sell the shares if and when the share price reached $60. She sold the shares at an average price of $58. Such agreements are typically a matter of record at Merrill Lynch and are known in the industry as a stop-loss order, but no such written agreement or order was ever found.

The investigations into insider trading activities and corporate scandals continued, but in mid-2002 the investigations suddenly changed focus. It was now Martha, America's most celebrated homemaker and a well-known, high-profile media mogul, who was the subject of headlines and the center of questions into insider trading. The U.S. Attorney General for the Southern District of New York, the Securities & Exchange Commission, and the House Commerce & Energy Subcommittee were all involved in the probe.

When the news of Martha's stock sale broke, her public relations firm issued a statement stating that the stock transaction was legal and also described the agreement she had with her broker to sell the shares if they dropped below $60 in value. The value of the stock of Martha Stewart Living Omnimedia Inc. dropped 54 percent and the company's profits plunged 45 percent in the third quarter of 2002.[9] Martha's personal wealth also plunged and, with a continuing probe and investigation hanging over her, she decided to give up her seat on the board of the New York Stock Exchange, something she was very proud of, and a decision that was personally difficult for her.

OBSTRUCTION OF JUSTICE AND SECURITIES FRAUD

In mid-September 2002, Martha received a notice from the Securities and Exchange Commission (SEC) indicating that civil insider-trading charges might be imminent. The SEC could also force her to step down as chairman and CEO of her company. The U.S. Attorney's office was also weighing charges of criminal insider trading, obstruction of justice, and fraud. Martha could face prison time if found guilty.[10] To many experts, the likelihood that Martha was guilty of insider trading was minimal. It was generally thought that the government would have a difficult time making the case against her because insider trading typically is said to occur when a high-ranking person within a company uses nonpublic information to buy or sell stock. Sam Waksal had already been found guilty of this aspect of securities law. In October 2002, Sam pled guilty to charges of attempting to sell his shares of stock and contacting family members to do the same after he learned that the FDA would not approve his company's application for the marketing and sale of Eribitux.

Sam's case was considered to be typical of insider trading violations, but Martha's case was not. Government officials argued that Martha had insider knowledge based on her relationship with Sam. Seth Taube, chair of securities litigation at the firm McCarter & English, and a former branch chief of enforcement at the New York regional office of the SEC noted: "Knowledge that another insider was selling has never been the basis for an insider-trading case."[11] Government prosecutors needed to prove that not only did Martha know ImClone insiders were selling the stock but she was also aware that the information was not provided to the general public. Government prosecutors could accuse Martha of lying to government investigators, obstruction of justice, or securities fraud, or they could impose civil charges. But the controversy, the headlines, and the stories that swirled about Martha were taking a toll, and she and her beloved corporation were suffering from being the target of an investigation.

Further adding to her worries, Kmart, an outlet for her home design products, had filed bankruptcy. Revenues and ad pages in the magazine were down, and her personal fortune had diminished. Prosecutors hadn't decided whether to indict her, and although she certainly didn't want an indictment, she did want a resolution. As part of an interview with Jeff Toobin, a former federal prosecutor, and a contributor to various news media outlets, in January 2003, Martha stated:

> (my) public image has been one of trustworthiness, of being a fine, fine editor, a fine purveyor of historic and contemporary information for the homemaker. My business is about home-making. And that I have been turned into, or vilified openly as, something other than what I really am has been really confusing. I mean we've produced a lot of good stuff for a lot of good people. And to be maligned for that is kind of weird."[12]

By May 2003, no formal charges had been filed. Sam had pled guilty and began serving prison time, and the politicians who had pursued Martha had moved on to other issues. Doug Faneuil, Peter Baconovic's assistant, cooperated in the investigation and pled guilty to a misdemeanor in September 2002. Despite a lack of formal charges, the case continued, although it seemed to be in limbo. Why was it taking more than a year to bring charges? As a result of the prolonged investigation, revenues in Martha Stewart Living Omnimedia were down. The share price of stock was also down, as were the number of ad pages in *Martha Stewart Living*. Federal prosecutors said the investigation was dragging along because of lack of cooperation by Martha and her legal team, which Martha, her attorneys, and Omnimedia aggressively denied. They noted they had provided documents and had answered all requests for information. Although an indictment against Martha would certainly be bad news, having the investigation in limbo was more damaging. Everyone wanted to move forward.

To the public, and certainly to Martha's fans, business was carried on as usual. In May 2003, Martha introduced a new line of furniture designs; and the company was moving forward to launch a new magazine called *Everyday Food,* which would be sold in grocery stories, and would have only a small reference to Martha on the cover or within the magazine.

By June 2003, a year after the investigation turned its attention toward Martha, the questions remained: Would she be indicted and would she do time if found guilty? What would happen to Martha Stewart Living Omnimedia if she served prison time? Despite the investigation and the questions, Martha maintained her composure and carried on with her business. She appeared on television and in print, and as far as the public was concerned, the lifestyle guru was carrying on as always. Behind the scenes of life as usual, the SEC, the FBI, and the U.S. Attorney's Office interviewed Martha about the sale of her ImClone stock. Throughout the meetings and interviews, Martha maintained her innocence and the truth of her story; the stock trade was based on a prior sell agreement with her broker. On June 4, 2003, after refusing to accept any plea bargain, or agreeing to any settlements that had been discussed, Martha was indicted for obstruction of justice and securities fraud by the U.S. Attorney's office in New York City. If found guilty of all charges, Martha could face 25 years in prison, $2 million in fines, and permanent damage to her reputation and to her beloved company. In addition to the criminal charges, the SEC also determined that they would seek to bar Martha from ever serving as an officer or director of a public company.

On the same day she was indicted, Martha stepped down as chairman and CEO of Martha Stewart Living Omnimedia. She was given the title of chief creative officer by the board of directors. Sharon Patrick, the chief operating officer, was made CEO, and Jeffrey W. Ubben, a board member and the largest outside shareholder, was named as chairman of the board. Martha's lawyers emphatically denied the charges and the board announced that they steadfastly stood behind her. "She is the company—more than the face of the company," said Ken Martin, managing director at Martin & Associates, an investment banking firm specializing in media. "People buy Martha Stewart products because they are Martha Stewart products."[13] Martha was being made a celebrity scapegoat, the lawyers and the board said, for more serious and certainly less glamorous corporate criminals. Her many fans thought she was being targeted because she was a highly successful, high profile, aggressive woman executive, and they vigorously defended her.

James Comey, the U.S. Attorney who brought the case against Stewart, said in a press conference that it would be "a tragedy" if it affected the fortunes of the Omnimedia shareholders and employees. But he added, "It's a tragedy that could have been averted if (Stewart) had only done what parents have told their children for decades—not to lie."[14] Comey also stated, "Martha Stewart is being prosecuted not for who she is but what she did."[15] An analyst at Morgan Stanley noted that Martha would never admit to any mistakes or defeat, and would always fight; that meant the company would have to fight the charges too.

After appearing in court, where she was fingerprinted and photographed, and where she listened to the charges against her, Martha confidently expressed her not guilty plea. The charges were now public and she was free to tell her side of the story. She and her team began an intensive public relations campaign. After a year of not publicly discussing the investigation or even admitting there was a probe, she was determined to let everyone know she was focused on business. The newspaper ads and the new Web site, marthatalks.com, were meant to generate enthusiasm with her fans and to highlight her belief that she was being targeted because she was a high-profile successful woman. She continued to host her TV show and continued to have a prominent presence in her magazine with her letters, photos, and her signature piece known as the monthly calendar.

For federal prosecutors, the task was to prove that Martha had repeatedly lied and attempted to cover up the circumstances surrounding the sale of stock. They contended that the sale agreement between Martha and Peter Bacanovic, her stockbroker, was a false alibi. Had Martha just sold the stock on her broker's advice, she likely would not have faced any investigation or have been indicted. Instead, she contacted Sam Waksal to ask about what was happening with ImClone and then sold her stock, thereby avoiding the subsequent losses after the FDA announced their intent to reject the biotech firm's application for approval of the anticancer drug. After the nine-count indictment for securities fraud and obstruction of justice was handed down, a trial date was set for January 12, 2004.

Martha, being Martha, continued writing scripts for her TV show, attending functions, and working on the magazine; she stated that she was busier than she had ever been. She said she always remained optimistic. Was she scared of the uncertainties of the future? Martha, who had built a successful empire from scratch, and who was one of the wealthiest and most watched women in the world answered: "I have not tried to stay out of the limelight. I go where I want to go and do what I want to do...I am not a fearful person."[16]

NOTES

1. Michael Schrage, "Martha Stewart," *Adweek*, 14 February 2000, 18.

2. Ibid.

3. Diane Brady, "Inside the Growing Empire of America's Lifestyle Queen: Martha Inc.," *Business Week*, 17 January 2000, 72.

4. Deidre McMurdy, "A Brand Called Martha," *Maclean's*, 4 December 2000, 49.

5. Christopher Byron, *Martha Inc.* (New York: John Wiley & Sons, 2003), 368.

6. Robert Slater, *Martha on Trial, in Jail, and on a Comeback* (Upper Saddle River, N.J.: Pearson Education, 2006), 25.

7. Ibid., 29.

8. Ibid., 31.

9. Julie Creswell, "Will Martha Walk?" *Fortune*, 25 November 2002, 121.

10. Ibid.

11. Ibid., 122.

12. Slater, *Martha on Trial*, 85.

13. Nanette Byrnes, Amy Borrus, and Lorraine Woellert, "The Martha Mess Becomes a Monster," *Business Week*, 5 June 2003.

14. Ibid.

15. Jyoti Thottam and Michael Weisskopf, "Why They're Picking on Martha," *Time*, 16 June 2003, 44.

16. Shawn Sell, "Martha Is Looking Up," *USA Today*, 2 September 2003, 01d.

Chapter 8

THE INDICTMENT, THE TRIAL, AND THE VERDICT

I am not guilty, but I feel sad, which is not a typical emotion for me. I keep saying why, why, why? This should never be a reflection on a business or a livelihood—it's terrible. For a creative person to be maligned like this is the worst thing that could happen. It takes away the joy.

—Martha Stewart

It is important to be realistic and to always remember that no matter how high you set your standards, no matter how intense your devotion to quality, no matter how detailed your business plan, stuff—I choose to use the more polite S word here—will happen.

—Martha Stewart

On a rainy day in June 2003, with a large umbrella shielding her from the downpour and her face from the onlookers, Martha emerged from her car and walked quickly into the courthouse. After hearing the charges against her, with a loud, emphatic voice, she pleaded not guilty. After entering her pleas, Martha was released without bail. Peter Bacanovic, her stockbroker, was also indicted on the same day and also pleaded innocent to all charges against him. Martha and Peter would be tried together. The trial date was set for January 2004.

In response to the indictment, Martha's lawyers responded: "(she) has done nothing wrong, and has become a celebrity scapegoat for more egregious, if less glamorous, corporate criminals."[1] Many of her fans agreed, saying Martha was being targeted as a woman executive who has made it in the business world typically dominated by men. On the issue of whether Martha was a celebrity scapegoat, her attorney, Robert Morvillo, said after the hearing, "Is it because she is a woman who has successfully competed in a man's business world by virtue of her talent, hard work, and demanding standards?"[2] James Comey, U.S. Attorney for the Southern District of New York said, "Martha Stewart is being prosecuted not for who she is but what she did."[3]

Martha had always been in the news; however, after the indictment the news coverage accelerated. She and Martha Stewart Living Omnimedia Inc. were now regularly part of the headlines and the subject of news stories everywhere. This news coverage and the reporters who seemed to be constantly shadowing her caused many headaches for both her and her company. Despite the charges and all the stories that swirled about her, she remained completely involved and focused on her company even though she had stepped down as CEO and president. But all the headlines, the news stories, and the seemingly constant parodies did take a toll on Martha and the company. The media had all but convicted her, concluding she was guilty of insider trading before she even went to trial.

By August 2003, just two months after the indictment, Martha Stewart Living Omnimedia announced quarterly losses and projected a loss for the year. President and CEO Sharon Patrick, who took over the position after Martha stepped down, said of the indictment at the time: "That although the company had been in the center of a sustained media firestorm for 16 months, we are better off than we were six months ago. I like to say we have gone from uncertainty to certain uncertainty because at least there will be a resolution." She reiterated that her goal was to support Martha and to maintain the company.[4] Sharon offered her support for her former boss, and Martha's fans remained steadfast that their lifestyle guru was innocent of all charges, but some experts remained unconvinced that neither Martha nor the company could rebound, even if in the end, she was found not guilty.

Since taking complete editorial control, Martha had been prominently featured on the cover and within the pages of the magazine. As a result of the indictment, Sharon and the board determined it was time to diminish Martha's visibility. As of September 2003, her popular monthly calendar no longer appeared in the magazine. Her "Remembering" column was deleted, and her name, always so prominently featured, was in smaller type on the cover. Adding to the downturn in her popularity and the damage to her and her company, several TV stations across the country moved her show to other time slots, noting declining viewers and lower ratings.

Still, Martha kept moving, involved in her business interests and focused on the business at hand.

In an attempt to show a "softer side" of Martha Stewart, she also granted interviews before the trial date of January 2004. In November, she appeared with Barbara Walters. Being careful not to discuss the specifics of the trial, she did discuss how difficult the previous months had been. When asked what had been the most painful part of the case, Martha responded to Barbara Walters: "I think a delay in a good life, a hiatus in a really fine existence. At my age, there's no time for an unexpected, undesirable, unwanted hiatus. None, one that you can't really control. It's difficult."[5]

In preparing for her trial, it was important that Martha appear to be softer, more sympathetic, someone more "of the people," even a victim, perhaps, of prosecutorial aggression, rather than harsh and difficult. Martha wasn't being tried for her management of her company or for insider trading as in other high-profile cases of the day. Instead, she was being tried for lying to federal prosecutors and for securities fraud. She was, however, facing a tough crowd of individuals who didn't believe in her innocence, and her friends and advisors believed that jury selection was nearly everything in this case.[6] She was facing a pool of individuals who, like many in America, had a low opinion of company executives, least of all powerful, aggressive women.

After months of preparation and nearly a year and a half of headlines and news stores, with diminished fortunes and a somewhat damaged reputation, and with a flurry of activity by Martha herself to show her control, her optimism, and her innocence, the trial finally began. On the first day, Martha arrived at the federal courthouse after reporters, television crews, supporters, and detractors had already gathered for a glimpse of the domestic diva, now seemingly the poster CEO for corporate scandals. Wearing high-heeled boots, a dark coat, brown trousers, and holding two bags, she emerged from her car, pushing her signature blonde hair from her forehead. Flanked by her security guard, she noticed the gathered audience and waved before entering the courthouse. Her trial, and that of her stockbroker, Peter Bacanovic, was finally underway, and although no one knew what was going through her mind, one could easily guess that she would much rather be anywhere else than be in the courtroom. For someone who had set such high standards for herself, who always felt invincible, and who had stated she "did what she pleased and did it with ease," the days ahead would likely be a nightmare.

The jury, eight women and four men, would decide whether Martha and Peter's explanations for the stock sale, the phone records, worksheets, and emails were plausible. A great deal hung in the balance, and much was at stake for the cultural icon, who for many days ahead, would enter through the metal detectors and make her way to the fourth floor, after facing a crowd mostly made up of supporters and reporters. Accompanying Martha was an entourage that included her daughter Alexis, her attorney, and the rest of her legal team.

THE TRIAL

The trial, presided over by U.S. District Judge Miriam Goldman Cedarbaum, commenced with opening arguments on January 27, 2004, and both the prosecution and the defense appeared to have challenges in making their cases. The Assistant U.S. Attorney, Karen Patton Seymour, argued why the government thought Martha and her stockbroker had obstructed justice, and how the case was about lying to cover up a tip that led to a stock sale. "The case is about truth," said Seymour, "The truth is what our nation's investigators are entitled to hear, to conduct their investigations fairly." Martha's lead attorney, Robert Morvillo, responded with a defense that attempted to play down the allegations and described Martha as a self-made woman from a poor family in Nutley, New Jersey, who "devoted most of her life to improving the quality of life for others."[7]

The prosecution was relying heavily on the testimony of their star witness, Doug Faneuil, Peter's former assistant at Merrill Lynch. As part of his plea bargain, Faneuil had admitted to changing his story while being interrogated by federal investigators, and he agreed to cooperate and testify. The defense would present evidence that Martha had suffered enough already. They would argue that Martha and her stockbroker would not spend so much time on a stock sale that netted approximately $50,000 when her total portfolio and her stake in her own company were far more important. According to them, the case was not really worth pursuing.

The media came to cover the trial every day. Although there were other scandals to cover, this seemed to be the best show in town. Martha's celebrity status, her well-known personality, her media conglomerate, and her success, all built from scratch, were on trial. Monday through Friday, Martha arrived at the trial, perfectly coiffed, impeccably dressed, and with an entourage that often included other celebrities such as Bill Cosby, Rosie O'Donnell, and her old friend from her stockbroker days, Brian Dennehy. Reporters covered the trial from diverse media outlets including *Time* and *Newsweek*, *Wall Street Journal* and *Forbes*, *People*, and *Vanity Fair*. Some reporters wrote as if she were guilty, and others knew their readership was fascinated by the prospect of a lifestyle guru going to jail. Allen Dodd-Frank of *Bloomberg News* at first determined not to cover the trial, but the case, he said, fascinated him. He wrote: "This was a celebrity trial that involved a businesswoman whose business was herself. It became apparent that she was a figure of enormous public interest."[8]

Mariana Pasternak, Martha's close friend and traveling companion to Mexico in December 2001,was scheduled to testify. She told the court that Martha told her the Waksals were selling their ImClone stock and that Martha had been given a stock tip. Also scheduled was Martha's personal assistant, Ann Armstrong, who took the message from Peter Bacanovic while Martha made her way to Mexico for a holiday vacation. All three had an immense influence with the jury and the outcome of the trial.

Doug Faneuil, a soft-spoken, 28-year-old, testified for three days in early February. As the former assistant to Peter Bacanovic, he was left in charge of Martha and Sam Waksal's stock portfolio while Peter was in Florida at the end of December 2001. On December 27, he took calls from Sam's family who all were eager to sell their ImClone shares. He called Peter, who responded by telling him to contact Martha. Doug took these instructions to mean he was to warn Martha to sell her shares. Not able to get in touch with Martha himself, he instructed Doug to expect her call. He asked whether he could tell her about Sam and was told emphatically that telling her was exactly the point. When Martha called, Doug told the court, he said to her, "Peter thought you might like to act on the information that Sam Waksal was trying to sell all his shares." She asked what the shares' price was and then ordered Doug to sell her shares.[9]

Initially, Doug Faneuil told investigators that there was a standing order at Merrill Lynch, an agreement between Peter and Martha that the stock should be sold if and when it reached $60 per share. Later, stating he had a guilty conscience, he recanted this story, and approached investigators admitting that he had lied and agreed then to testify against Peter and Martha. In return, Doug was charged with a misdemeanor for initially misleading the government. According to trial observers, the three-day testimony was electrifying and the carefully developed plan to soften her image was "blown to bits." What he had to say riveted the court. He told stories of his prior contacts with Martha, causing some observers in the courtroom to snicker, and at one point to erupt in laughter. Doug told of his prior contacts with Martha, stating she sounded "kind of like a lion roaring underwater." He added, "Martha yelled at me again today but I snapped in her face…Baby put Ms. Martha in her place!"[10] Martha appeared at one time to be close to tears and at another point, ashen. Some trial observers thought it was Doug's testimony that refuted Martha's carefully cultivated softer image before the trial.

When Martha instructed Doug to sell her shares of ImClone, Doug testified that he offered to send an email confirming the stock sale to Ann Armstrong, her personal assistant. Martha, he related, became irate and answered: "Absolutely not, you have no right to tell Ann Armstrong about my personal transactions."[11] The only way for Martha to overcome Faneuil's damaging testimony was to testify on her own behalf. At this point in the trial, no one knew if she would, in fact, do just that.

Another key witness at Martha's trial was Ann Armstrong, Martha's personal assistant since 1998. Testifying on Monday, February 9, 2004, she described her phone conversation with Peter Bacanovic on December 27, 2001, which included taking the message, "Peter Bacanovic thinks ImClone is going to start trading downward." Ann testified that she and Martha spoke about each other's Christmas, and that she thanked Martha for the plum pudding she had sent to her. Ann then covered her eyes and began to sob. After recessing for the day, Ann continued her testimony the next morning when she again discussed the phone conversation with Martha. Ann was then asked about events on January 31, 2002, five days before Martha was to meet with federal investigators. Ann testified that Martha asked her to send the phone messages from December 26 through January 7 to Martha's attorney's office. She then stated that Martha wanted to see the message log on the computer. Ann testified that, after scrolling to the messages for December 27th, "Martha saw the message—'Peter Bacanovic thinks ImClone is going to start trading downward,' from Peter; she took the mouse, put the cursor at the end of the sentence, highlighted it back to the end of Peter's name, and then started typing over it." She further testified that Martha sat at Ann's desk, and replaced the message with 're imclone,' all lowercase...and that Martha had then spoken with her son-in-law, attorney John Cuti, who then met with Ann that evening to discuss putting the message back in its original form."[12]

Unfortunately, Ann stated, she didn't know how to do this because she didn't remember what the original message said. She also told the court that Martha had asked that the message be changed back to its original form instantly.[13] Questioned by Martha's attorney, Robert Morvillo, Ann testified that Martha had never asked her to lie or conceal the truth. To the jury, it appeared that Martha had changed the phone message and quite possibly tried to destroy evidence.

The third and last witness called to testify was Mariana Pasternak, Martha's longtime friend and traveling companion to Mexico in December 2001. Mariana, who was Martha's neighbor in Westport, Connecticut, told the court they had been friends for 20 years. She related how the two spoke daily and often vacationed together in the years leading up to

December 2001. Mariana testified that she saw Martha make a phone call during their fueling stop in Texas before flying on to Mexico for their vacation. She said that although she couldn't recall the content of the call, she remembered that Martha had raised her voice. Mariana then related that when they were in their hotel suite on December 30, 2001, three days after Martha had sold her ImClone stock, they discussed Sam Waksal. She related that Martha had said he (Sam), "was selling or trying to sell his stock...his daughter was selling or trying to sell his stock."[14]

The attorneys for Martha's codefendant, Peter Bacanovic, tried to claim that her testimony was hearsay; however, Judge Cedarbaum overruled the motion, allowing the testimony to proceed, as the testimony didn't directly concern Bacanovic, Martha's broker. When asked if she remembered anything else, Mariana replied that yes, there was one other statement Martha made to her: "Isn't it nice to have brokers who tell you those things!"[15]

At this point in the testimony, the day in court ended, leaving the jury with much to think about. This testimony seemed to conflict Martha's assertion that she hadn't been aware that Sam wanted to sell his shares, and that her request to sell her ImClone stock was based on a prearranged sales agreement with her broker. The next day, February 20, 2004, Martha's attorney, Robert Morvillo, questioned Mariana. He asked her if she was sure about Martha's statement about broker's information. She replied: "It's fair to say I don't know if it was a statement Martha made or if it was a thought in my mind."[16] She further stated that it was her best belief that Martha had made the statement. Despite her doubts, she did give the jury information to consider during their deliberations.

As the government prosecutors got close to resting their case, many wondered if Martha would testify. Martha was certainly an excellent communicator and polished speaker. Taking the stand could help her case, according to some experts. Prior cases involving corporate scandals and high-profile individuals, however, had shown that testifying on one's own behalf could easily backfire, or could undermine credibility. If she didn't take the stand, this could be a sign to the jury as an admission of guilt. By not having either Martha or Peter testify, this could be a sign that the defense was confident that the government had not proven their case. Although she had no legal obligation to testify, many wondered if hearing her speak, listening to her side of the story, perhaps even apologize and say that it was never her intent to break the law, would have greatly helped her case.

In the end, the decision was made that neither Martha nor Peter would testify. The only witness called to defend her against charges of lying to investigators was attorney Steven Pearl. He testified about notes he took at a meeting held in February 2002. Federal investigators accused Martha of lying at that meeting when she told them that she wasn't sure if her broker left a message for her on December 27, 2001, the day of the stock sale. Steven Pearl's testimony was in response to the testimony given by Martha's assistant, Ann Armstrong, in which she told the court Martha had viewed the computer phone log from December 27, 2001 and altered the record of the message from her broker, Peter Bacanovic. Ann then testified that Martha immediately ordered her to restore the message to its original form. According to the notes provided by Attorney Pearl, he couldn't recall what Martha had said during the interview and that his role was to take notes to capture the substance of the meeting, rather than a verbatim record. To many experts, the testimony was confusing and of little use to the defense.

Martha did receive a break from the judge. In early March 2004, Judge Cedarbaum threw out the charge of securities fraud, the most serious charge on her indictment; charges of conspiracy, obstruction of justice, and two counts of lying to investigators remained.

THE VERDICT

After two hours of jury instructions, the jury received the case on March 3, 2004. The trial that began on January 20 was nearing its end. It took three days for the jury to convict, although the jury decided Martha's fate after one day, and then moved on to deliberations for Peter Bacanovic. On Friday, March 5, 2004, Martha, dressed in her requisite dark pantsuit, showed little emotion as Judge Cedarbaum repeated the word "guilty" four times. Alexis, sitting behind Martha, as she had every day throughout the trial, dropped her head in her hands and then was motionless. The verdict for Martha's codefendant, Peter Bacanovic, was guilty on four of five counts.

The scene outside was frenzied as the crowd waited for news. The first sign of the verdict was given as reporters streamed from the courthouse waiving red scarves, a signal for a guilty verdict. After leaving the court-room, with Alexis at her side, Martha acknowledged the crowd gathered outside the building with a slight smile. A few hours later, Martha posted a statement on her Web site: "I am obviously distressed by the jury's ver-dict but I continue to take comfort in knowing...that I have the enduring support of my family and friends. I will appeal the verdict and continue to fight to clear my name. I believe in the fairness of the judicial system and remain confident that I will ultimately prevail." According to Robert

Slater, in his book *Martha on Trial, in Jail, and on a Comeback,* the first version of her message stated that she took comfort in "knowing I have done nothing wrong." These words were removed at the insistence of her attorney, believing this could anger the sentencing judge, or be considered a snub to the judge and the jury.[17]

Although many agreed that Martha had flaws and that she was arrogant and mean and needed to always be in control, many also acknowledged that she did change American culture, that she set standards, built a business from scratch, and had became one of the wealthiest individuals in America. A living brand, Martha was admired, mocked, parodied, and constantly watched. She set trends and made homemaking a worthwhile way to spend one's time. Her vision had built a business that began in the kitchen of her home and eventually became a multimedia conglomerate. No one could say her legacy wouldn't live on, but what would become of Martha Stewart Living Omnimedia? The experts were divided. So much was wrapped solely on her. And while her message might be diluted for a while, and while she wouldn't be quite as ubiquitous as before, many agreed that she would be back, that she would indeed prevail. Others weren't quite so sure.

When Omnimedia went public in 1999, there was much fanfare and great expectations. But investors had long worried over what would happen if Martha could no longer run the company, for whatever reason. After the verdict, shares of Omnimedia fell nearly 23 percent.[18] Her daytime television show was taken off the air with no date announced for its return. And although she wasn't required by the SEC to do so, Martha resigned from the board of directors. Many experts wondered if the company could survive, and still others thought it could, based on a balance sheet that showed cash reserves and little debt. During the investigation, the company made serious efforts to downplay Martha's role within the company and this would continue after the verdict was announced. Both Martha and the company she loved so much were seriously damaged by the verdict and even if she won the appeal, considered a long shot by many experts, could she and the company recover?

Reeling from the verdict, Martha knew she had to look deeply into what had happened. She needed to consider that if changes were necessary, she would need to be ready to make them. She spoke with friends and family, including her daughter Alexis, her mother, who was almost 90 years old and was heart broken over the verdict, and her brother Frank, whom she hadn't spoken with for several years. Martha wasn't someone to retreat into obscurity, and she vowed that she would comeback.

Martha's sentencing was scheduled for July 17, 2004. Few believed she would get jail time, but Martha couldn't be sure. In the courtroom, she stood before Judge Cedarbaum, her voice breaking, and told the judge she was afraid that her life would be "completely destroyed." She asked the judge to "remember all the good I have done." And she told the Judge she was entrusting her future to her "competent and experienced and merciful hands."[19]

Martha's attorney, Robert Morvillo, asked the Judge to give Martha probation and community service. He said, "She has brought a measure of beauty to our everyday world with refined color schemes, floral arrangements, and culinary delights. She has stood for the values of quality and making products as perfect as possible."[20] Judge Cedarbaum noted she had received more than 1,500 letters from supporters, appealing for leniency. Nevertheless, she felt a prison term was appropriate because "lying to government agencies during the course of an investigation is a very serious matter, regardless of the outcome of the investigation . . . I believe that you have suffered, and will continue to suffer enough." However, the judge said she had not lost sight of the seriousness of the crime of which Martha had been convicted. She had decided, nonetheless, to be lenient given that Stewart had no record of previous criminal conduct.[21]

THE SENTENCE

Judge Cedarbaum sentenced Martha to five months in jail to be followed by five months of house arrest; she also required Martha to pay a $30,000 fine. The judge recommended that Martha serve her sentence at a minimum-security facility in Danbury, Connecticut. While the case was under appeal, Martha was free. Peter Bacanovic was also sentenced to five months in prison, five months of home confinement, and was ordered to pay a fine of $4,000.

Just after sentencing, Martha confronted the media on the courthouse steps. "Is this on?" she asked, grabbing a microphone. "That a small personal matter has been able to be blown out of all proportion and with such venom and gore, I mean, it's just terrible. I have been choked and almost suffocated to death. I'll be back. I will be back."[22]

Just after her sentencing, Martha appeared in an interview with Barbara Walters. She compared herself to Nelson Mandela and added, "I didn't cheat the little people. We're all little people."[23]

On October 8, 2004, Martha began serving her sentence at the Alderson Federal Prison for Women in Alderson, West Virginia. She had decided that serving her prison sentence was the quickest way to end what she called her nightmare. This was the best career move yet. Serving her sentence voluntarily and giving up the notion of appealing her conviction was the best way to save herself and her company. Accompanied by her lawyers and members of her board of directors, she called a press conference on September 15 and said:

> I have labored long and hard to build this company and I love the company, my colleagues, and what we create very much. I cannot bear any longer the prolonged suffering while I and my legal team await vindication in the next step of the legal process, the appeal. And although I and my attorneys firmly believe in the strength of that appeal, recently delays and extensions have now made it abundantly clear that my appeal will not be heard until some time next year. So I have decided to serve my sentence now, to put this nightmare behind me and get on with my life and living as soon as possible. The only way to reclaim my life and the quality of life of all of those related to me with certainty, now, is to serve my sentence, surrender to the authorities, so that I can quickly return as soon as possible to the life and the work that I love. I hope, too, that I will be able to begin serving my sentence in the very near future, because I would like to be back as early in March as possible in order to plant the new spring garden and to truly get things growing again.

Martha ended her announcement with a joke, saying that she had been walking through Manhattan when a man spotted her and said, "Oh, she's out already...I hope that my time goes as fast as that. I'll see you next year."[24]

NOTES

1. Jyoti Thottam and Michael Weisskopf, "Why They're Picking on Martha," *Time*, 16 June 2003, 44.

2. Robert Slater, *Martha on Trial, in Jail, and on a Comeback* (Upper Saddle River, N.J.: Pearson Education, 2006), 96.

3. Ibid.

4. Shawn Sell, "Martha Is Looking Up," *USA Today*, 2 September 2003, 01d.

5. Slater, *Martha on Trial*, 105.

6. Greg Farrell, "Jury Selection Is Everything," *USA Today*, 20 January 2004, 01b.

7. Greg Farrell, "Stewart Painted as Liar, Honest Victim," *USA Today*, 28 January 2004, 01b.

8. Slater, *Martha on Trial*, 117.

9. Michele Orecklin and Simon Crittle, "Oh, My God, Get Martha on the Phone," *Time*, 16 February 2004, 48.

10. Ibid.

11. Barney Gimbel and Keith Naughton, "A Diva in Distress," *Newsweek*, 16 February 2004, 36.

12. Slater, *Martha on Trial*, 145–146.

13. Ibid., 146–147.

14. Jessi Hempel, "The Martha Trial: With Pals Like This…" *Business Week Online*, 20 February 2004.

15. Ibid.

16. Slater, *Martha on Trial*, 152.

17. Ibid., 174.

18. Ibid., 179.

19. Ibid., 184.

20. Ibid., 184–185.

21. Ibid.

22. Keith Naughton and Barney Gimble, "I Will Be Back," *Newsweek*, 26 July 2004, 40.

23. Ibid., 41.

24. Slater, *Martha on Trial*, 194–195.

Chapter 9

PRISON AND PLANNING THE COMEBACK

I had spent my career and built my company's reputation working hard to bring good things to as many people as possible. And yet a personal stock trade was threatening to destroy everything: my successful television show, my much-loved magazine and book projects, a nationally syndicated radio show, a vibrant product design and merchandising business, and a highly creative staff that was never at a loss for ideas. Wall Street valued us, our growth was good, and our prospects were extremely bright. But one thing remained constant. From day one of this horrible nightmare, I received enormous numbers of letters and emails—supportive, positive messages from my viewers, readers, listeners, and customers. Partners such as Kmart stood firmly behind my company.

—Martha Stewart

The personal decision to voluntarily go to jail and serve her sentence, despite a pending appeal, was likely one of the most difficult decisions of Martha's life. Martha was indeed a strong woman; however, she did not know what she would face in prison. She did not know how the guards and inmates would treat her or who would protect her if things became difficult. Yet, this strong, smart, business-savvy woman made her decision, and to many, it may have been one of the most brilliant decisions of her life, or at least of her comeback.

After hearing the jury's guilty verdict, Martha tried her best to resume her life while deliberating her future. She exercised, she visited friends, and she went to baseball games. Slowly, she came to the decision that to begin again, to be once again the lifestyle icon she was before, she needed to put the trial and her conviction behind her. For this reason, Martha opted to serve her prison sentence rather than to continue to fight the legal battle. Her decision was hailed as sophisticated and savvy. On October 8, 2004, six days after holding the press conference where she was so obviously supported by her legal team, members of her board of directors, and the woman who had been chosen as her successor, Sharon Patrick, Martha was ordered by Judge Cedarbaum to begin serving her sentence. The Federal Bureau of Prisons announced that she would serve her sentence at the federal prison in Alderson, West Virginia, denying her request for a prison located in Danbury, Connecticut, where she would be nearer to her home and her mother, Martha Kostyra.

To Martha, it was likely, in part at least, a decision made to help win back her fans, and put the public back on her side. Martha was intent on making a comeback, as she had earlier vowed, and her decision helped her do just that. She told writer Patricia Sellers of *Fortune* magazine: "There wasn't one lawyer who worked on my case who advised me to go to prison. They said it would look bad, it would harm my case. It would tell people that I was guilty." But Martha insisted that she knew all along what she had to do: serve the time and get it over with so that she and her company could move on. "My life is my business. My business is my life. I've said that a thousand times. I had to do it because I knew it would change things—jigger a change—in the company."[1]

The announcement took some of the uncertainty about the direction and management of Martha Stewart Living Omnimedia. The stock value rose on the announcement and experts agreed that advertisers would likely make their way back to *Martha Stewart Living* magazine after some had pulled their ads and others had cut their spending during the trial. Many had applauded Martha's decision, but others weren't sure it meant anything at all, especially as she never showed remorse or offered any apology.

Martha's long-time supporter, author and *Vanity Fair* magazine columnist, Dominick Dunne, who covered the trial extensively, said: "Speaking as a friend and admirer of Martha Stewart, I think she has made a very wise decision to serve her time without waiting for the appeal process. Get it over with. It is very disheartening to live with a legal dark cloud over your head. I thought she handled her announcement with grace, class and style."[2]

Janice Schrettner, a member of *USA Today's* Pop Culture Panel, said she was less impressed. "Even though it is still brave to do this, somehow the business motivation behind it lessened my respect for what she is doing. On another note, it annoys me that she still does not show any regret about what she did, is not in the least apologetic, and in fact seems very defiant."[3]

With the difficult and some say brave decision to go to jail and serve her time, Martha's comeback effort was underway. With her prison time awaiting her, Martha signed a television development agreement with Mark Burnett, the TV producer behind *Survivor* and *The Apprentice*. His reputation as the man behind wildly successful TV shows certainly added to Martha's ability to make an effective comeback. The effect of having an agreement with Mark Burnett also signaled a return for Martha and her personality-driven brand at Omnimedia. It remained to be seen whether Martha and Omnimedia could rebound while Martha served her time and after her release. Martha and many experts believed that although her comeback might be difficult, America always loves a comeback, and Americans, especially the legion of fans who are loyal to Martha to the very end, are forgiving and don't believe in permanent humiliation. After all, Martha is too smart and too driven to not once again be the domestic diva, the cultural icon, and the living brand she had been before. She wanted to be on top and really no one could stop her.

Martha announced in July that she was not afraid of what lay ahead and she stated emphatically that she would be back.[4] And few doubted her assertion. After the press conference announcing her decision, and after the announcement of the development agreement with Mark Burnett, the Omnimedia board announced it was replacing Sharon Patrick with Susan Lyne as the new CEO. Lyne was the founder of *Premiere* magazine, a former president of ABC Entertainment, and the woman who had developed the hugely popular *Desperate Housewives* television show for ABC. Martha also installed Charles Koppelman on the board of directors for Omnimedia. Koppelman was the former advisor to Michael Jackson, the chairman of Steve Madden shoes after the founder of the shoe company went to jail, and he was also known as an advisor to many celebrities including Barbra Streisand and Billy Joel.

A few days later, Kmart, which continued to sell Martha Stewart brand items, announced a merger with Sears, which prompted talk of whether the retail giant would continue Martha's agreement for Martha Stewart products in stores across the country. As a result of all these announcements, Omnimedia's stock rose more than 27 percent over three weeks, as did Martha's net worth.[5]

THE INCARCERATION

On October 8, 2004, Martha entered Alderson Federal Prison as inmate 55170–054. The prison was nicknamed "Camp Cupcake," suggesting that it was a relatively easy place to spend an incarceration. For her part,

Martha referred to Alderson Prison as "Yale," so that she would never have to say the word prison, and she often added that she had always wanted to go to Yale.

On the day she arrived, the town of Alderson was abuzz in anticipation of Martha's arrival, and local business boomed. The media arrived and took residence at the one motel in town. Martha had hoped to enter prison quietly, so her picture would not be in newspapers or magazines, always reminding the public of her crime and her incarceration. Martha issued the following statement that day:

> Today marks the beginning of the end of a terrible experience, and I am now one step closer to getting this awful time behind me. I deeply appreciate all of the support I have received throughout this ordeal from those people close to me and from many thousands of well-wishers around the world. While I am serving my sentence, my attorneys will continue to pursue my appeal. They believe it is a strong appeal that presents very serious legal issues, and the brief will be filed shortly with the court. Over the course of the next five months, Martha Stewart Living Omnimedia will be in the good hands of its talented management team and creative staff, and every day I am away, I will look forward to rejoining them to pursue my life's work. That work is all about creating beautiful, practical, and educational magazines and television programs as well as inspiring and useful products for the home. I'll see you again in March.[6]

The prison, originally a collection of cottages in the mountains of West Virginia, has a long history dating back to the 1920s as the nation's first federal women's prison. Singer Billie Holiday spent a year there for a narcotics violation and Lynette "Squeaky" Fromme, a member of the Charles Manson family, spent time there for pointing a gun at President Gerald Ford. Over the years, the prison has changed from a series of cottages where inmates lived in their own rooms, to one of large dormitories housing as many as 500 inmates. There is no privacy, and male guards can walk in on women as they use the bathroom and verify head counts by pulling off bed covers while the inmates sleep. The prison population at Alderson Prison is largely made up of minority, low-income women, many with a history of sexual and drug abuse. Like many other prisons in the United States at the time, the prison suffers from budget constraints and overcrowding that affect rehabilitation and vocational programs.

When Martha arrived at Alderson, she was fingerprinted and strip searched. Her clothes and valuables were sent back home. She traded her chic designer clothes for prison issue shirts and pants; for use in kitchen work, she was also issued black, steel-toed shoes; she was provided with underwear, bras, and socks. Martha has often said that she only sleeps a few hours per night, so her 6 A.M. wake up wasn't unusual; however, her breakfast of cereal, toast, and sometimes eggs, might have been. Her lunch typically consisted of a cold sandwich and her dinner, a warm main entrée, certainly not haute cuisine, or what Martha would likely have eaten.

The 7 1/2-hour workday began at 7:30 A.M. In the evenings, inmates were allowed to watch TV, read, play games, and exercise until lights out. Martha's mother, Martha Kostyra, said, "They all have to buy the clothes they are going to wear. Can you imagine? If you want extra food you pay for that, too. Most of the food is government surplus; that's why it's so bad."[7]

Martha was given a job cleaning the administration office, including the toilets, for which she earned 12 cents per hour. She had requested a job in the prison kitchen. She said of her job: "I did the vacuuming and the cleaning of the machines—I'm good at that. When the envelop-opening machine in the post office broke, I was the only one who could fix it."[8]

The prison food—certainly food Martha wasn't at all used to—was heavy on carbohydrates and often consisted of "bad meat." Martha said, "It would have been great to tell them that I'm a vegetarian. I sign up for vegetarian meals when I fly." She lost 20 pounds by skipping dinner in the prison cafeteria and using a microwave to cook meals with her fellow inmates. They made meals using pasta, kale, dandelion greens, and other vegetables from the prison garden that was tended by the inmates. "I got relaxed," Martha said, "I felt calmer. I felt better. My stress level, I'm sure, was cut in half."[9]

Martha worked out in the prison gym each morning, and practiced and taught yoga to her fellow inmates. Quite possibly, what was most difficult about being in Alderson Federal Prison was being cut off from her business. She had no Internet access and was not allowed to con-duct business with visitors or by telephone. She was limited to 300 minutes of phone time per month, which proved difficult for her. "I told the warden, 'I use that in a day! He told me, 'You have to make an adjustment.'"[10]

Martha was able, however, to write while in prison. Her book, *The Martha Rules*, inspired, she said, by a seminar she gave to inmates about starting businesses, was outlined while there. She also wrote the introduction to television producer Mark Burnett's book *Jump In!*

Stories about Martha's prison life slowly leaked from Alderson. The stories were meant to show Martha's new softer, more human side, and not the untouchable, disagreeable side. One story described how Martha smuggled seasonings out of the prison kitchen inside her bra. The *New York Post* headline was "Nice Spice Rack."[11] Another story told how Martha commiserated with her fellow inmates about the food and how she was teaching yoga and providing advice for starting businesses and counseling inmates on how to reconnect with family and pursuing interests. For their part, many of the inmates eagerly protected Martha, shielding her from the reporters and photographers that often surrounded the prison grounds.

Martha was allowed visitors four days a week, with the visits either in the morning or afternoon hours. Martha's daughter, Alexis, visited nearly every weekend, driving for 10 hours from Connecticut. Other visitors included Susan Lyne, who replaced Sharon Patrick as CEO of Omnimedia, and Charles Koppelman, an important member of Martha's comeback team and a board member of Omnimedia. Martha was allowed to listen to them describe what was happening within the company; however, she wasn't allowed to make any decisions. Nevertheless, she listened carefully and her mind raced with ideas for what she would do after leaving prison.

THE PLANNED COMEBACK

Despite the stories and all the careful, strategic planning by Martha's comeback team, the corporation remained in a rather fragile state. Omnimedia announced a record loss in revenues in 2004, which was nearly 10 times the loss it suffered in 2003.[12] A contributing factor to the downturn was the other magazines that were competing for the same audience that were doing well in the marketplace. Still, many experts and certainly her board of directors were confident that by serving her sentence voluntarily and by showing a softer side of Martha, and with the number of fans who remained loyal and the expressions of sympathy that abounded while she was in prison, Martha's carefully choreographed comeback would succeed.

By early December, there were two important announcements: Martha would have a new syndicated daytime TV show, and she would be doing her own version of *The Apprentice*. There had been a lot of media hype about what type of show Mark Burnett and Martha would do, and the buzz continued about whether Martha would be like Donald Trump in his version of the popular television show. The idea of a prime-time reality television show had been proposed during the trial. For a Martha Stewart version of *The Apprentice*, Donald Trump had to be persuaded, as he was initially unsure of whether a spin-off was wise. Trump, as co-owner and the driving force of the show, had veto power: "When the idea was first broached, I said to myself, 'I wonder if that's too much exposure for the show?'" He was finally convinced after being shown how spin-offs from other shows such as *CSI* and *Law & Order* actually boosted ratings of the original shows. Trump, a friend and supporter of Martha, said: "That she should be in jail and O.J. Simpson is playing golf in Florida is ridiculous. But she took it standing up. There were no tears. No dropping to the ground. I've seen very strong men who can't handle that."[13]

The new shows were slated to debut in the fall of 2005, and it was expected that Martha would interact with audience members and guests. Martha, of course, was full of ideas and eagerly awaited her release in early March 2005. The comeback of Martha Stewart was on track and in constant motion.

On her last night in prison, March 3, 2005, almost a year after she was found guilty of conspiracy, obstruction of justice, and two counts of lying to investigators, the inmates gave her a farewell party. Meanwhile, a small crowd of Alderson residents gathered at the Greenbrier Valley Airport, about 17 miles from the prison grounds, hoping to catch a glimpse of one of their most famous neighbors, to say good-bye to Martha. One resident held up a sign that wished her good luck and asked her to come back for a visit. Of course, there were also members of the media there to report on the domestic diva leaving prison. Nancy Grace, a commentator for CNN, watched Martha, in her poncho, jeans, and high-heeled boots, smile and wave to the crowd. She told her audience that Martha looked stylish and had a smile as she boarded her plane. She added, "Martha Stewart is making a comeback…She's back…taking off for another chapter in her life."[14] Keith Naughton, a CNN panelist and writer for *Newsweek*, said: "She just looked much more casual than we've seen her before. She just looked very relaxed and really started waving and smiling and looked warm. Even throughout her whole trial, she never looked sort of warm and comfortable as she does right now. Maybe that's just part of the image makeover or maybe that indicates a real change…She looks fabulous."[15]

Shortly after 2 A.M. on March 4, 2005, wearing a hand-knitted gray poncho that a prison friend had made for her and accompanied by her daughter Lexi, Martha left Alderson Federal Prison for Women a free woman, flying by private jet bound for Westchester County Airport and home to her 153-acre estate in Bedford, New York, known as Cantitoe Farms. She would be under house arrest for five months and confined to one building, although she would be able to leave for up to 48 hours each week for work, shopping, and doctor's appointments. Until August, Martha could not walk about on her estate. Her probation officer would visit randomly, and she would have to wear an electronic ankle bracelet at all times. Still, the Martha comeback, carefully orchestrated by her team, was underway.

In her book, *Martha Rules*, which she outlined while in prison, and published in 2005, Martha said her time at Alderson was more positive than she had anticipated. She said, "It is no secret that I am accustomed to being in control—of my life and of my company. What became all too apparent during my confinement was how many, many women are not in control of their lives or what happens to them." Martha wrote that she made it a priority to understand the women incarcerated at the prison and that they did the same for her. She wrote that she was fortunate to have so many friends and family visiting her, and that many of her fellow inmates had no one. While at Alderson, Martha said she missed her home, her animals, travel, fresh food, and managing her business; but that while in prison she made new friends, and had time to read fascinating books. She said, "I also gained a new appreciation for the complexity of every single person's situation...It is important to be realistic and to always remember that no matter how high you set your standards, no matter how intense your devotion to quality, no matter how detailed your business plan, stuff...will happen."[16]

NOTES

1. Patricia Sellers, "Remodeling Martha," *Fortune*, 31 October 2005.

2. Greg Farrell and Theresa Howard, "Stewart Takes Steps to Reclaim 'Good Life,'" *USA Today*, 16 September 2004, 01b

3. Ibid.

4. Robert Slater, *Martha on Trial, in Jail, and on a Comeback* (Upper Saddle River, N.J.: Pearson Education, 2006), 204.

5. Sellers, "Remodeling Martha."

6. Robert Slater, *Martha on Trial*, 204.

7. Lloyd Allen, *Being Martha* (Hoboken, N.J.: John Wiley & Sons, 2006), 181.

8. Sellers, "Remodeling Martha."

9. Ibid.

10. Ibid.

11. Slater, *Martha on Trial*, 211.

12. Keith Naughton, Johnnie L. Roberts, Karl Gude, and Lisa Bergtraum. "Martha Breaks Out," *Newsweek*, 7 March 2005, 36–44.

13. Ibid.

14. Slater, *Martha on Trial*, 220.

15. Slater, *Martha on Trial*, 219.

16. Martha Stewart, *Martha Rules* (New York: Martha Stewart Living Omnimedia, 2005), 156–157.

Chapter 10

HOME AGAIN, THE COMEBACK, NEW BUSINESS VENTURES

When I think of Martha Stewart, I see smart and strong. And I see lists, because she makes them all: powerful people, powerful women, influential entrepreneurs. The secret to her success is that she's Martha. Indomitable Martha.

—Donald Trump[1]

On March 4, 2005, Martha left Alderson Federal Prison for Women by private jet, loaned to her by a good friend, and returned home to Cantitoe Farms, her 153-acre estate in Bedford, New York, about an hour north of New York City. This was her homecoming weekend, and this was where the comeback for the domestic doyenne would be launched. To many who saw her leave prison and arrive home, Martha looked fit and re-laxed. Waving to the reporters and photographers that lined her fence, she smiled and told those gathered that there was no place like home. The first hours of her freedom were spent relaxing and enjoying family and friends. Later she went outside to chat with the reporters and served them hot chocolate and freshly baked cranberry-walnut bread. She was unsure at first if she had already violated the strict rules of her home confinement. But her probation officer gave her a 72-hour grace period before she was to be fitted for the electronic ankle bracelet, one of the requirements of her five-month house arrest.

During her house arrest, her movements would be severely restricted. She would be allowed to leave her estate six days per week, for work, medical appointments, and to attend religious services. The total time outside her home could not exceed 48 hours per week, and for one full day each week she was required to stay inside the house. Another condition of her home confinement was that she could not walk the grounds of her estate. After five months of house arrest, she would be on probation for 18 months, and she would be required to report to a probation officer. She would have to ask for and receive permission to travel. No one could disagree that Martha looked forward to August 2005, when the terms of her house arrest would come to an end and she could cut off the ankle bracelet, her tether to her 153-acre estate. Martha left prison ready to begin her comeback with a detailed to-do list, despite the strict constraints of her court-ordered home confinement.

Although her comeback had been carefully planned and orchestrated since before entering Alderson, it did not include holding a news conference after her prison release. Martha knew that at a press conference, she would be asked about her prison stay and whether she should have apologized for her actions. She wanted to put the prior five months behind her and to offer an apology, or to even speak about offering an apology, would conflict with the ongoing appeal of her sentence. Instead of a press conference or interviews, she released a short video of her first weekend home that featured her in the kitchen with her mother. The purpose was to show Martha back in her kitchen, on familiar turf, doing what she loves and does best.

Martha's list of items to be checked off during her home confinement included planning for the next gardening season, writing for *Martha Stewart Living* magazine, supervising the remodel of some of the buildings on her estate, and checking in periodically with her probation officer, who was required to preapprove her schedule. Margaret Roach, editor of *Martha Stewart Living,* wrote in a letter to readers, "The anticipation of these new beginnings—a new house, a new garden—has certainly sustained her spirits. Based on visits with her at Alderson, W. Va., and our letters back and forth these past month, I can tell you she is, indeed, ready to get planting, having ordered seeds and made extensive to-do lists, just as she would have done in any winter."[2] A spokesperson for Omnimedia stated, "We are eager to have her back at work, and know how much she looks forward to coming home."[3]

Martha's prison release meant she would again be drawing her monthly salary of $75,000 from the corporation, Martha Stewart Living Omnimedia.[4] According to the company's regulatory filings, as of March 2005, Martha owned 29.1 million shares of Omnimedia stock. When she was convicted in March 2004, the price per share of the stock was as low as $8.70; in anticipation of her release from prison, the per share value of the stock on the first of March 2005, was $35.35, giving Martha's shares a value of over $1 billion.[5]

Even though sales were still down from previous years, and there were operating losses compared to previous annual profits, the stock Martha Stewart Living Omnimedia was doing very well, and as a result, at least financially, so was Martha. Despite the rise in the stock price, the Martha Stewart brand was considered tainted by many marketing experts, the result of the negative publicity during the investigation and the trial itself, as well as because of increased competition from new magazines and products for the home entertaining and decorating market. In April, however, just one month after her release from prison, *Time* magazine published their annual list of the world's most influential people. The list included heads of state, leaders and revolutionaries, artists and entertainers, and scientists and thinkers. The list of builders and titans included Martha Stewart, alongside Apple's co-founder Steve Jobs and billionaire businessman and media magnate Rupert Murdoch.[6] For someone just released from prison, and after fighting an indictment and waging a widely publicized court battle, Martha's influence, by making this important list in an important and widely read periodical, was apparent and certainly remarkable.

Many experts agreed that Martha's stay in prison had increased her popularity, or at least garnered enough sympathy for her to maintain her fan base. To be sure, the residents of Bedford, New York and Westchester County were ready for their famous neighbor to return home. They were used to seeing Martha in the hardware store or at a local restaurant during the five years she owned the estate. On the homecoming weekend, they all appeared to be "Martha ready," which meant they were ready for the influx of reporters, photographers, and fans they knew would come in force. Although reporters covering her return outnumbered the supporters, the community welcomed her home. One resident and business owner said, "It doesn't seem like it's bothered anyone. The consensus is it hasn't been too much of an inconvenience. It'll pass. It always does. We all do our own thing here." Another resident said, "She's like anyone else in town. The locals give them (celebrities) their space. We leave them alone. We respect their privacy."[7]

On Monday, March 7, a few days after her release and her homecoming weekend, Martha addressed the staff of Martha Stewart Living Omnimedia in New York. Her announcement included her plans for a new vision for Omnimedia, saying that the company would be more in touch with ordinary people, not the upscale readers and viewers she had targeted in the past. She added that the company would focus not only on the methods used in entertaining and cooking but on why readers and viewers should deem such activities important.

Perhaps this new vision came in part from her experiences at Alderson. Her time in prison was more than difficult, but it did offer certain positive experiences and also gave Martha new perspectives. According to Lloyd Allen, in his book *Being Martha*, the women Martha met in prison would never leave her mind and heart. She wrote on her Web site just after leaving prison:

> Someday, I hope to have the chance to talk more about all that has happened, the extraordinary people I have met here and all that I have learned. I can tell you now that I feel very fortunate to have had a family that nurtured me, the advantage of an excellent education, and the opportunity to pursue the American dream. You can be sure that I will never forget the friends that I met here, all that they have done to help me over these five months, their children, and the stories they have told me.[8]

The April 2005 issue of *Martha Stewart Living* magazine was one facet of Martha's comeback. The cover featured a bowl of daffodils that announced spring and the season's renewal; it was a renewal for Martha, too. Besides a spring photograph, the cover also featured a portrait of Martha with a headline, "Welcome home, Martha." Her presence in the magazine had been much less visible after her March 2004 conviction. Her column "Ask Martha" and her monthly personal essay had disappeared. In celebration, and certainly to announce Martha's return to the magazine and to Omnimedia as a whole, the April 2005 issue once again included her personal column. A new two-page column was also added, entitled "From My Home to Yours." The regular and very popular monthly calendar that was always featured before her conviction was absent, as was her popular "Remembering" column, where Martha reminisced about days gone by. Just after announcing her vision and her resolute return to business, *Forbes* magazine published its list of world's billionaires, and Martha made the list for the first time. The magazine estimated her net worth at $1 billion and put her in last place, at 620th, tied with 39 other billionaires.[9]

NEW BUSINESS VENTURES INCLUDING *MARTHA* AND *THE APPRENTICE*

Not letting her ankle bracelet or the terms of her house arrest deter her, Martha jumped right into the planning of her daytime talk show to be called *Martha*. One aspect of what made this show different from the previous show was the format. The earlier show, with its how-to segments and cooking and domestic advice, had been taped from her home at Turkey Hill. The new talk show was to be taped before an audience in a new carefully designed studio, fully equipped with a kitchen and garden. The show was also to include appearances from celebrities. Lisa Wagner, the show's producer, said that they were working to produce something very different and the new concept felt right. She said the show always had its core viewers, but that they wanted to reach out to more new viewers. Martha, she said, was back in a role that felt a lot less perfect, and lot more fun, and that the new show was a how-to show, but had more entertainment. They wanted to show Martha's sense of humor, something that people who knew her well were quite familiar with. The new show, she added, was going to be relatable to many more people than the earlier show.[10]

While the new shows were being planned and new corporate visions being announced, Martha Stewart Living Omnimedia announced financial results for the first quarter of 2005. It included an operating loss and posted less revenue than the same quarter of 2004. Susan Lyne, president and chief executive officer, said in the announcement: "2005 has started off as we expected with the company seeing momentum both from the strength of our brand and Martha's return. Importantly, Martha's return has energized the entire Company, and customers have enthusiastically welcomed her home. We thank them, our corporate partners and advertisers for their continued support."[11] She further stated that she saw early signs of improvement in the core publishing business, as well as positive circulation trends and ad pages in the magazine. She noted the new and exclusive arrangement with Sirius Satellite Radio and the soon-to-be distributed how-to DVDs, all of which was intended to make content more accessible to loyal customers and reach to new audiences. The announcement also included information about trends and what might impact the Company's forecasts that included adverse reactions by consumers, advertisers, and business partners to the publicity related to Martha's trial and conviction, and the pending SEC enforcement proceedings against Martha. It also included information about downturns in economies, the loss of Martha's services during incarceration, changes in consumer patterns, and the reception by consumers of new product introductions.[12]

As part of the comeback and her new vision for Omnimedia, Martha also announced a 24-hour program on Sirius Satellite Radio to be called Martha Stewart Living Radio, which would feature cooking, gardening, and entertaining programming. In a statement about the new venture,

Martha noted that it would be the first "around the clock" channel devoted entirely to areas of interest for women. In early May, Martha offered a preview of her new talk show, *Martha,* to a group of ad executives that was scheduled to debut in September. The response to the viewing was enthusiastic. The executives, from markets all across the country, felt Martha had a unique style and was showing a more humble spirit. They thought audiences would respond positively to the new spirit of the show and felt Martha showed a renewed strength and commitment.

Amid all of the planning, press releases, meetings, and official comeback of the domestic diva, one of the biggest days in the life of Martha Stewart was to be August 10, 2005. This was the day the home confinement would end and the ankle bracelet, Martha's tether to the trial, to prison, to her house arrest, would be cut off. Unfortunately, the day came and her house arrest was extended by three weeks. Although no reasons were publicly given for the extension, August 31 was to be the next big day. Late that same month, Martha held a news conference in New York to provide the details of her new shows and a tour of the new set where her new show would be filmed. She told those in attendance that the new show would not be a talk show, as there was no couch anywhere, but an entertainment how-to show with a live audience. Not providing any details about *The Apprentice* to the reporters, she did tell one reporter that five minutes after midnight on August 31, she would take off the anklet, and once again, have her freedom. She then thrust her leg up in the air and showed off the bracelet. Martha's probation would continue for another 18 months, but she would be getting more freedom and would return to work on a full-time basis without having to watch the clock, or remain on her estate throughout the week. Its removal marked the true beginning of Martha's comeback.

Although the strategies for reinventing Martha had been in the works for a long time, Martha and her team designated September 2005 as the "official" comeback. In September, the new talk show would debut, the radio show was scheduled to go on the air in the fall, and Martha's version of *The Apprentice* was also scheduled to debut on the TV network. Martha was going to be everywhere again.

The relationship with Sirius Radio was important, and the new daytime talk show was highly anticipated, but it was Martha's version of Donald Trump's *The Apprentice* that seemed to create the most excitement, or at least the most talk. Scheduled to debut in September 2005, the planning of the prime-time spin-off was planned before leaving for prison. Just as the trial was ending, in March 2004, Martha met with reality television producer Mark Burnett. Known as the guru of reality shows, Mark was behind the popular show *Survivor* and felt strongly that a Martha Stewart version of Donald Trump's *The Apprentice* would show Martha's sense of humor, her spontaneity, and her business acumen, while giving her positive exposure to a skeptical public. Martha was receptive to the proposal, especially at a time when the trial was nearing its end and someone was reaching out to her and believed in her and her future. Donald Trump, however, had to be convinced that it was the right idea at the right time. Trump was co-owner of his show and had power to veto any spin-off arrangement. He said at the time that he wondered if the idea meant too much exposure for the show.[13] Mark Burnett, for his part, showed how other spin-offs were successful and had actually boosted the ratings of the original show. Jeff Zucker, NBC TV Chief, was behind the proposal for another *Apprentice*, featuring Martha, saying, "The fact is, the American public loves a great comeback. And her story is even more compelling now."[14]

Neither Mark Burnett nor Donald Trump felt the signature "you're fired" response to the contestants was appropriate for Martha. All thought it was important to show another side of Martha and chip away at the icy, demanding demeanor she had always been known for, and having this kind of heavy handed response would only reinforce this reputation. The idea now was to show a softer side to the domestic diva and to reinforce her comeback and her new vision. Trump, it was believed, could get away with being heavy handed; Martha, it was determined, could not. As well, the boardroom setting, as in Trump's *The Apprentice*, wasn't appropriate for Martha; however, neither was firing a potential Martha Stewart protégé while in the kitchen. Martha saw her version of *The Apprentice* as "the vehicle that would get her company back on its feet." She said: "*The Apprentice* is meant to let viewers see, in addition to being a how-to teacher, that I am also a good boss-manager. I want them to see that part of our world—especially now, because it is very important to revitalize this fantastic company, to get people back on track about what we are and what we do here."[15]

In Martha's version, the apprentice would be chosen from 10 women and 6 men, ranging in age from 22 to 42, who would compete for 13 weeks by completing tasks in Martha Stewart-related fields that included publishing, entertainment, and fashion, the last an area that Martha had always avoided being involved. Charles Koppelman, Omnimedia's chairman, and the man at Martha's side when she emotionally announced she would go to prison voluntarily, and Martha's daughter Alexis, were a part of the program that would be taped while Martha remained under house arrest. While both Charles Koppelman and Alexis Stewart would serve as advisors, especially as Martha would have to remain at her home in

Bedford, New York, Martha assured her audience that she would make all decisions about who would stay and who would leave each week. There was great speculation about how Martha would fire the contestants each week. What phrase would she use after Trump had made his "You're fired" part of the American lexicon?

On September 21, 2005, the first episode premiered, opening with a short biography of Martha. She told her viewers that she was the first female self-made billionaire in America. She said she would be in complete charge of the show, and each week a contestant would be eliminated from the competition to win a $250,000 per year position at Martha Stewart Living Omnimedia. Speculation of how the firing would go finally ended with the first contestant being told, "You just don't fit in," a kinder phrase, an easier firing. Martha then sent a personal note to the contestant. She has always been the impeccably mannered diva.

In an interview for *Time* magazine on September 19, 2005, Martha was asked how she differed from Donald Trump and if she felt she was "incredibly tough to work for." She answered:

> Donald loves to fire people. I find it an extremely unpleasant exercise. I have other people do it for me...Somehow I have managed to build a very fine company with a very fine work force filled with people who are still there from the earliest days. Many of my executives have worked with me since the beginning. I can be fair and decisive and encouraging as well as demanding, and those are the characteristics you'll see on *The Apprentice*.[16]

After the premier, reviews for *The Apprentice: Martha Stewart* weren't especially positive. Diane Brady, in *Business Week Online*, noted that it "feels more like a trip to finishing school than a trial by fire." She noted that what made Trump's version so successful was the "dog-eat-dog demeanor and chewing out the contestants for their various faults." She stated that Martha "has morphed into a mother figure who nurtures more than she needles."[17] The appeal seemed to be Martha Stewart and the experts agreed that to make the show successful, she would have to put more of who she is into the show, perhaps be edgier and more assertive and dwell less on the new softer side of the self-described household name and living brand. Ratings for the show were below what was expected by NBC. The value of the stock of Martha Stewart Living Omnimedia fell after the first show. Neither Martha nor Omnimedia held any financial interest in the show. Despite the show's low ratings after a great deal of hype and high expectations, however, investors remained positive about Omnimedia's stock even though the company had been losing money since Martha's indictment. As a result, Martha's financial stake, with her 91 percent ownership, suffered; however, her ambitious plans for her comeback, which included *The Apprentice*, a new daytime talk show, a satellite radio show, and how-to DVDs, kept her busy, challenged, and moving forward, despite warnings that she could be overexposed and that her persona would be oversaturated in the eyes of the public.

For his part, Mark Burnett signed a consulting agreement with Omnimedia, giving him a stake in the company. Martha also received $500,000 in compensation from Omnimedia in addition to her $900,000 annual salary and annual bonuses.[18] This was on top of her annual salary, her perks from the company, and annual bonuses. Martha's financial arrangement for her version of *The Apprentice* and the stock purchase agreement negotiated by Mark Burnett were expenses of Omnimedia. Thus it was important to everyone concerned that the new prime-time show succeeded. Unfortunately, the show flopped. It was one of the lowest rated shows on network television in prime time. This further affected Omnimedia's bottom line, causing the stock price to fall, losing a third of its value since the show premiered. Martha's comeback after prison seemed to be losing the expected luster and steam. The NBC network quickly lost faith in Martha. They had switched the time slot, putting the show up against the wildly popular ABC show *Lost*, dooming it altogether. Mike Paul, a New York public relations expert said: "Viewers aren't connecting with Martha's *Apprentice* because they sense she is holding back from being herself. She's trying to be something she's not...she has a reputation as a tough boss. I've been in an elevator when Martha is berating her employees, and let me tell you, it's not pretty. But it's not boring either."[19]

When asked about her experience on *The Apprentice*, Martha answered: "I thought I was replacing The Donald. It was even discussed that I would be firing the Donald on the first show." The blame, as she saw it, was not with her performance or her personal brand being overexposed, but with the overexposure of *The Apprentice* itself. It wasn't until after she left prison that she learned that Trump's show would remain on the air. She described the experience as a triumph saying, "We're getting six to seven million viewers a night. Guess what, that's damn good. People walk away from the show thinking, 'what a nice company that is,' and boy, do they do good things."[20] Martha felt she was getting extremely good exposure on prime time just when she needed it the most.

The comeback continued, despite the show's poor performance, and Martha, the media mogul, the multimedia star, was undeterred. As she has always done in her life, she kept moving on. As part of the official September 2005 comeback, and coinciding with the debut of *The Apprentice*, Martha and her team had long planned a new daytime talk show with a new format, a fresher look, with a revitalized Martha at the helm. The new show, much different from her show that was always taped in her own kitchen at her home on Turkey Hill Road, was carefully planned as a part of the reinvention of the new Martha. While *The Apprentice* generated a great deal of publicity, it received less attention from investors and business experts because it was considered a temporary show and was outside of both Martha's and Omnimedia's core businesses. The real Martha and what the domestic diva does best were to be featured once again. On her release from prison, Martha jumped right into to getting ready for her show. Lisa Wagner, the producer of the show, described the new show as something exciting, and that viewers would see something very different. The intent, she said, was to reach out to new viewers and to show that the new show would be relatable to many more people. She added that the mood on the set was upbeat, and that the new studio was the largest live TV studio ever built. Martha, she assured everyone, had a lot of confidence in her key people. The most important thing to Martha, Lisa said, was that the show delivered valuable content, and that this was never going to change, and that Martha's viewers and readers always expect quality.[21]

On September 12, *Martha*, described as a lifestyle-oriented show, and an updated version of her previous show, premiered on NBC. The new show, broadcast live to more than 100 cities across the United States, had a studio audience and celebrity guests and would be rebroadcast later in the day on the Discovery Channel. The filming was over three mornings and two afternoons each week on a set specifically designed for the program, complete with a full kitchen and greenhouse resembling Martha's own home kitchen at her Bedford estate. Martha also planned to mingle with people outside the studio and to surprise a viewer by visiting her home and assisting with the preparation of a meal. When asked if the live broadcast and a participating audience and celebrity guests would make her nervous, Martha responded that she looked forward to being spontaneous and described the show as a how-to show with entertainment.

When Martha left Alderson Prison and boarded the private jet to return home, she wore a hand-knitted poncho, made especially for her by a fellow inmate. The studio audience wore the same poncho on the new show. Martha explained: "When I left prison, I wore the poncho…a very industrious company that sells yarn put the pattern on their website, and one million designs were downloaded. They let us put an invitation on their site asking anybody who made a poncho to come be in the audience of the show. We got between 10,000 and 15,000 responses within an hour, and just over 100 of those people will be at the show."[22] The poncho, Martha added, was going to be saved for her personal archives.

The initial responses to the show by ad executives were positive, but even after the network had sold the show to nearly 85 percent of the markets in the country, the new show did little to help the drop in the value of the stock of Omnimedia caused by the poor ratings of *The Apprentice*.[23] After months of hype, the prime-time show was a catalyst for the stock's decline. As well, many experts wondered if the two shows would result in an oversaturation of Martha Stewart. Would the public tire of seeing the ubiquitous Martha? Omnimedia executives responded that the magazine was doing very well, and that the daytime talk show was off to a great start, adding that the company wasn't worried about the poor response to *The Apprentice*. Media experts and Martha's fans agreed. They wanted Martha to be Martha again, to be what made her a household name and doing what she does best. The show was continually compared to the prime-time show, and as a result, ratings were positive, but not stellar. Even so, after the first season, it was picked up for a second season.

THE MARTHA RULES

A third aspect of the official comeback of Martha Stewart was the publication of her new book titled *The Martha Rules: 10 Essentials for Achieving Success as You Start, Grow, or Manage a Business*, published in October 2005. The book's dedication reads: "Alexis Stewart, and all other young entrepreneurs with hopes and dreams for a fine future." In the acknowledgments, Martha wrote that there were many people who inspired, taught, influenced, and supported her while she built her own entrepreneurial venture. She added: "The construction of Martha Stewart Living Omnimedia has been a meaningful and exciting journey—not just for me, but for each and every colleague who has spent time with me, designing and erecting and maintaining a fine, worthwhile, productive American dream."[24]

Martha outlined the book while in prison and was inspired by a seminar she did for fellow prisoners on entrepreneurship. In October 2005, appearing on NBC's *Today Show* to discuss the book, Martha told Katie Couric that she was happy to give advice to fellow inmates during her five months at Alderson. She said:

> They have a lot of time to think and plan for the future...In many of these institutions, there are no consultants, there are

no real teachers there to help these women, some of whom are incarcerated for 20 years...I was so happy to be able to be of use and be helpful and give advice because their minds are working 24 hours a day, just like our minds are working." She added that her book tells readers to fill a void with something's that needed, and not to sacrifice the quality of a big idea, and "build your business around something that you are inherently passionate about.[25]

In the book, Martha writes that many women, young, middle-age, and older, had dreams of starting a business when they were released and many came to her seeking advice, telling her of their passions and ideas. She studied the plans and was struck by how complicated and expansive they were. Being an experienced mentor, she was glad to give advice; however, she also said she was required to be fair, critical, and even blunt. She encouraged planning, investing, partnering, and careful, thoughtful research in her seminar to the inmates.

To the readers of the book, she suggests the following: building businesses around something interesting; focusing attention and creativity on basic things; creating a business plan to stay true to a "big idea;" teaching so that you can learn; conveying what is special about the business; knowing that quality is something to strive for; hiring employees with integrity, optimism, and generosity; searching for advisors and partners who complement skills and beliefs; evaluating and assessing a situation and focusing on the positive and staying in control; knowing that there is a difference between a risk and a change and taking advantage of opportunities; and listening intently, learning new things every day, innovating, and becoming an authority. She also outlines a list of assessing business ideas that includes questions for the entrepreneur to develop and refine ideas for a successful business.

As part of Rule #2, in which she suggests focusing attention and creativity on basic things, things that people need and want, and looking for ways to enlarge, improve, and enhance a "big idea," she writes: "Looking back on my journey as an entrepreneur, it is quite clear, to me at least, that everything I have ever done has stemmed from a desire to provide as many people as possible with products and services that they absolutely need and absolutely want. Homemaking, homekeeping, has been a topic of enormous interest to me, and I really can and do determine what my customers need and want by what I need and want."[26]

Martha was given a $2 million contract to write the book for Rodale Books, who understandably believed in her and her ability to write, to sell books based on the success of her prior books; they believed that she would be back as popular as ever. Initially the book sold well and appeared on *The New York Times* bestseller list. Unfortunately, by December 2005, two months after the book was released, sales were disappointing.

NEW BUSINESS VENTURES FOR MARTHA AND FOR MARTHA STEWART LIVING OMNIMEDIA

The comeback plans didn't end with *The Martha Rules,* and it wasn't only about the daytime show or Martha's version of *The Apprentice.* The careful, strategic plan also included a continuing relationship with Sears to carry her line of home furnishings, the how-to DVDs with Warner Home Video, a music deal with Sony BMG, the $30 million deal with Sirius satellite radio, a partnership with KB Home to build Martha Stewart-branded residential communities, a new line of paint with the home improvement store Lowe's, a line of photo products with Eastman Kodak, a partnership with Federated Department Stores for a line of upscale home merchandise, and two new magazines, *Blueprint* and *Body + Soul.* None of these plans and deals happened by chance. Everything was deliberately calculated and carefully plotted by Martha and her personally selected comeback team before serving her prison sentence, and likely before her conviction.

On August 7, 2006, Martha reached an agreement with the Securities & Exchange Commission to settle her insider-trading accusation, concluding a five-year battle. The settlement called for Martha to pay $195,000, which covered her gains from trading and penalties. Also, the agreement prevented her from serving as chief financial officer or director of any public company for a five years. It did not preclude her from retaining her title or impede her from her influence over Martha Stewart Living Omnimedia. In a statement, Martha said: "This brings closure to a personal matter and my personal nightmare has come to an end."[27]

Martha once adamantly said she would continue her fight to clear her name and always maintained her innocence of all charges against her. She also said she intended to once again be the leader of the company she founded, after resigning that post just after her indictment. While the August 7, 2006 agreement precludes her from accomplishing this goal for five years, everyone can expect that at the end of that period, she will more than likely again be at the helm of her company. In the meantime, she has creative control and continuing influence.

MARTHA'S CONTINUING INFLUENCE
AND THE FUTURE

Martha Stewart built her empire based on the packaging of a distinctive American style. She was and continues to be nearly evangelical in her advice and what she believes is the ideal, the ultimate level of perfection. She came to believe that there is a certain way to plant a tree or paint a wall; there is a certain way to mix a drink or serve brunch. And Martha has always believed that anyone can learn and do what they want to do. She put it so aptly in the September 2000 edition of Oprah Winfrey's magazine, O, when she said: "I can almost bend steel with my mind. I can bend anything if I try hard enough. I can make myself do almost anything."[28]

Three generations have known and watched Martha and her meteoric rise and swift downfall. What will she do next? Her fans watch, Wall Street anticipates, and the public cheers, jeers, smiles, and even frowns. Martha Stewart's life is always filled with drama and controversy, leaving her fans and detractors to question, wonder, clap, and dream. She makes her own rules and goes at a speed few can match. Standing in her way isn't at all wise. After Martha's time at Alderson Prison, her revitalization was completely a tribute to a woman who has a sharp strategic sense and acute business acumen. Martha knows only one way to do business and that is full speed ahead. She never had and didn't need another plan for returning to her status as a lifestyle trendsetter, the high priestess of perfection, a cultural icon or a living brand. Perhaps Martha put it best when she said: "It's totally out of desire and totally out of belief that—not that I am essential, but that I am still a vibrant, wise human being with great dreams for the future, great hopes for the future, a great team to work with and a really great company to be involved with. I mean this is my life."[29] For her legions of fans, that truly is a "good thing."

NOTES

1. Donald Trump, "Martha Stewart," *Time*, 18 April 2005, 72–73.

2. James T. Madore, "This 'Halfway House' Goes All the Way," *Charleston Daily Mail*, 1 March 2005.

3. Ibid.

4. Jennifer Medina and Abigail Sullivan Moore, "Martha's Privacy Seems to Be Everyone's Business," *The New York Times*, 13 March 2005, 14.

5. Brett Arends, "A Billion for Being in Prison," *Boston Herald*, 1 March 2005.

6. Adi Ignatias, "The People Who Influence Our Lives," *Time*, 18 April 2005, 46–49.

7. Medina and Sullivan Moore, "Martha's Privacy," 14.

8. Lloyd Allen, *Being Martha* (Hoboken, N.J.: John Wiley & Sons, 2006), 212.

9. Robert Slater, *Martha on Trial, in Jail, and on a Comeback* (Upper Saddle River, N.J.: Pearson Education, 2006), 226.

10. Allen, *Being Martha*, 208–209.

11. "Martha Stewart Living Omnimedia, Inc. Announces First Quarter 2005 Results," *PR Newswire*, 26 April 2005.

12. Ibid.

13. Keith Naughton, et al., "Martha Breaks Out," *Newsweek*, 7 March 2005, 36–44.

14. Ibid.

15. Slater, *Martha on Trial*, 246.

16. Michele Orecklin, "10 Questions for Martha Stewart," *Time*, 19 September 2005, 8.

17. Diane Brady, "Martha's Apprentice Needs an Edge," *Business Week Online*, 22 September 2005.

18. Robert Barker, "A Flop for Martha's Investors," *Business Week*, 26 September 2005, 26.

19. Kim Khan, "TV Flop Takes Toll on Martha's Stock," *CNBC Market Dispatches*, 27 October 2005.

20. Patricia Sellers, "Remodeling Martha," *Fortune*, 31 October 2005.

21. Allen, *Being Martha*, 209–210.

22. Orecklin, "10 Questions for Martha Stewart," 8.

23. Naughton, et al., "Martha Breaks Out," 36–44.

24. Martha Stewart, *The Martha Rules* (New York: Martha Stewart Living Omnimedia, 2005), iix.

25. "Martha Stewart Shares Her Recipe for Business Success," *The Associated Press*, 11 October 2005.

26. Stewart, *The Martha Rules*, 24–25.

27. Thomas Landon, "Stewart Deal Resolves Stock Case," *The New York Times*, 8 August 2006, C1.

28. Christopher Byron, *Martha Inc.* (New York: John Wiley & Sons, 2003), 45.

29. "You Can't Keep a Good Diva Down: 'I Mean This Is My Life.'" *Financial Times Ltd.*, 30 August 2005.

APPENDIX

MARTHA STEWART BOOKS

Stewart, Martha, and Elizabeth Hawes. *Entertaining*. New York: C. N. Potter: Distributed by Crown Publishers, 1982.

Stewart, Martha. *Martha Stewart's Quick Cook*. New York: C. N. Potter: Distributed by Crown Publishers, 1983.

———. *Hors d'oeuvres: The Creation and Presentation of Fabulous Finger Foods*. New York: C. N. Potter Publishers, 1984.

———. *Martha Stewart's Pies & Tarts*. New York: C. N. Potter. Distributed by Crown Publishers, 1985.

Stewart, Martha, Elizabeth Hawes, and Christopher Baker. *Weddings*. New York: C. N. Potter: Distributed by Crown, 1987.

———. *Martha Stewart's Quick Cook Menus: Fifty-two Meals You Can Make in under an Hour*. New York: C. N. Potter. Distributed by Crown Publishers, 1988.

Stewart, Martha, and Christopher Baker. *The Wedding Planner*. New York: Potter: Distributed by Crown, 1988.

Stewart, Martha. *Martha Stewart's Christmas Entertaining, Decorating & Giving in the Holiday Season*. New York: C. N. Potter, 1989.

———. *Martha Stewart's Gardening Month by Month*. New York: C. Potter, 1991.

———. *Martha Stewart's New Old House*. New York: Clarkson Potter, 1992.

Source: Denver Public Library WorldCat—a catalog of books, videos, DVDs, Web resources and other library materials owned by libraries worldwide. http://www.denver.lib.co.us/wc-bin/fs-worldcat.

———. *Martha Stewart's Hors d'Oeuvres: The Creation and Presentation of Fabulous Finger Foods*. New York: C. N. Potter, 1992.

———. *Holidays: Recipes, Gifts, and Decorations, Thanksgiving & Christmas*. New York: Oxmoor House, 1993.

———. *Holidays: Recipes, Gifts and Decorations, Thanksgiving & Christmas*. New York: Clarkson Potter, 1993.

———. *Special Occasions: The Best of Martha Stewart Living*. New York: Oxmoor House, 1994.

———. *Special Occasions: The Best of Martha Stewart Living*. New York: Clarkson Potter, 1994.

———. *Martha Stewart's Menus for Entertaining*. New York: Clarkson Potter/Publishers, 2002, 1994.

———. *Martha Stewart's Menus for Entertaining*. New York: Clarkson Potter Publishers, 1994.

Stewart, Martha, and Dana Gallagher. *Martha Stewart's Menus for Entertaining*. London: Ebury Press, 1994.

Stewart, Martha. *What to Have for Dinner: The Best of Martha Stewart Living*. Birmingham, Ala.: Oxmoor House, 1995.

———. *Handmade Christmas: The Best of Martha Stewart Living*. New York: Clarkson Potter, 1995.

———. *The Martha Stewart Cookbook: Collected Recipes for Every Day*. New York: C. Potter Publishers, 1995.

———. *Special Occasions: The Best of Martha Stewart Living*. New York: Clarkson Potter, 1995.

———. *New Martha Stewart Cookbook*. London: Ebury Press, 1996.

———. *How to Decorate: The Best of Martha Stewart Living*. Birmingham, Ala.: Oxmoor House, 1996.

———. *What to Have for Dinner: The Best of Martha Stewart Living*. New York: Clarkson Potter, 1996.

———. *Martha Stewart's Healthy Cooking*. New York: Clarkson Potter Publishers, 1996.

Stewart, Martha, Hannah Milman, and William Abranowicz. *Great American Wreaths: The Best of Martha Stewart Living*. Birmingham, Ala.: Oxmoor House, 1996.

Stewart, Martha. *Great Parties: Recipes, Menus, and Ideas for Perfect Gatherings: The Best of Martha Stewart Living*. Birmingham, Ala.: Oxmoor House, 1997.

———. *Christmas with Martha Stewart Living*. New York: C. Potter, 1997.

———. *Martha Stewart's Healthy Quick Cook: Four Seasons of Great Menus to Make Every Day*. New York: Clarkson Potter, 1997.

———. *Christmas with Martha Stewart Living*. New York: Martha Stewart Living Omnimedia, 1997.

Stewart, Martha. *Great Parties: Recipes, Menus, and Ideas for Perfect Gatherings: The Best of Martha Stewart Living*. New York: C. Potter, 1997.

Stewart, Martha, and Amy Conway. *Good Things: The Best of Martha Stewart Living*. Birmingham, Ala.: Oxmoor House, 1997.

———. *Good Things: The Best of Martha Stewart Living*. Little Rock, Ark.: Leisure Arts, 1997.

Stewart, Martha. *Decorating Details: Projects and Ideas for a More Comfortable, More Beautiful Home*. New York: Oxmoor House, 1998.

———. *Christmas with Martha Stewart Living. Decorating for the Holidays: Volume 2*. Birmingham, Ala.: Oxmoor House, 1998.

———. *Decorating for the Holidays*. New York: Omnimedia, LLC., 1998.

———. *Decorating Details: Projects and Ideas for a More Comfortable, More Beautiful Home: The Best of Martha Stewart Living*. New York: C. Potter, 1998.

———. *Desserts: Our Favorite Recipes for Every Season and Every Occasion*. New York: Clarkson Potter, 1998.

———. *Martha Stewart Living Special Issue: Clotheskeeping*. New York: Martha Stewart Living, 1998.

Stewart, Martha and Hawes, Elizabeth. *Entertaining*. New York: C. Potter, 1998.

Stewart, Martha, and James A. Baggett. *Arranging Flowers: How to Create Beautiful Bouquets in Every Season*. New York: Clarkson N. Potter, Inc., 1999.

Stewart, Martha, and Kathleen Hackett. *Crafts and Keepsakes for the Holidays*. New York: Clarkson Potter, 1999.

Stewart, Martha, and Susan Spungen. *Martha Stewart's Hors d'oeuvres Handbook*. New York: C. Potter, 1999.

Stewart, Martha. *Arranging Flowers: How to Create Beautiful Bouquets in Every Season: The Best of Martha Stewart Living*. New York: C. Potter, 1999.

———. *Desserts*. New York: Random House International; London: Hi Marketing, 1999.

———. *Favorite Comfort Food: A Satisfying Collection of Home Cooking Classics*. New York: Clarkson Potter, 1999.

———. *Favorite Comfort Food: A Satisfying Collection of Home Cooking Classics*. New York: Omnimedia LLC, 1999.

Martha Stewart Baby Special Issue: A Supplement to Martha Stewart Living. New York: Martha Stewart Living, 2000.

Stewart, Martha. *Holiday: Halloween*. New York: Martha Stewart Living, 2000.

———. *The Martha Stewart Living Cookbook*. New York: Clarkson Potter, 2000.

Stewart, Martha, and Amy Conway. *Parties and Projects for the Holidays*. New York: Clarkson Potter, 2000.

———. *Christmas with Martha Stewart Living: Parties and Projects for the Holidays*. New York: Martha Stewart Living Omnimedia: Oxmoor House, 2000.

———. *Halloween—the Best of Martha Stewart Living*. New York: Random House International London: Hi Marketing, 2001.

———. *Martha Stewart's Favorite Cookie Recipes*. New York: Martha Stewart Living Omnimedia, 2002.

———. *Classic Crafts and Recipes Inspired by the Songs of Christmas*. New York: Random House International; London: Hi Marketing, 2002.

———. *The Martha Stewart Living Christmas Cookbook*. New York: Clarkson Potter, 2003.

———. *Martha Stewart's Baking Handbook*. New York: Clarkson Potter Publishers, 2005.

———. *The Martha Rules: 10 Essentials for Achieving Success as You Start, Build, or Manage a Business*. Emmaus, Pa.: Rodale. Distributed to the trade by Holtzbrinck Publishers, 2005.

———. *Martha Stewart's Baking Simple Suppers*. New York: Random House. Enfield: Hi Marketing [distributor], 2005.

———. *Martha Stewart's Homekeeping Handbook: The Essential Guide to Caring for Everything in Your Home*. New York: Clarkson Potter Publishers, 2006.

MARTHA STEWART MAGAZINES

Blueprint
Body + Soul
Everyday Food
Good Things
Kids: Fun Stuff to Do Together (2002–2006)
Martha Stewart Baby (2001–2003)
Martha Stewart Living
Special issues including the annual *Holiday Cookies*
Martha Stewart Martha (Japan, 2001)
Martha Stewart Weddings

MARTHA STEWART COLUMNS

Distributed to newspapers through the United States via *The New York Times* Syndicate

Ask Martha
Martha Stewart Living
Martha Stewart Weddings
Martha Stewart Everyday Food

MARTHA STEWART ON TELEVISION AND ON THE RADIO

Martha (syndicated, daily)
Everyday Food (PBS, weekly)
Petkeeping with Marc Morrone (syndicated, weekly)
Martha Stewart Living (reruns broadcast on Style Network; no longer in first-run production)

Martha Stewart Living Omnimedia operates a satellite radio channel, *Martha Stewart Living Radio*.

MARTHA STEWART WEB SITES

http://www.marthastewart.com
http://www.Marthasflowers.com

MARTHA STEWART MERCHANDISING

Martha Stewart Living Omnimedia additionally offers various home goods through its mass-market Martha Stewart Everyday brand in Kmart stores throughout the United States, and at Sears Canada. Furniture and paint are part of the company's specialty-retail oriented Martha Stewart Signature brand, in partnerships with Bernhardt Furniture Company, Fine Paints of Europe, and Sherwin-Williams. The company announced in April 2006 its plans to develop a new, upscale merchandise line for Federated Department Stores scheduled for rollout in 2007 at Macy's stores nationwide. Source: http://en.wikipedia.org/wiki/Martha_Stewart.

FURTHER READING

Allen, Lloyd. *Being Martha*. Hoboken, N.J.: John Wiley & Sons, 2006.

Arends, Brett. "A Billion for Being in Prison." *Boston Herald*, 1 March 2005.

Brady, Diane. "Martha's Apprentice Needs an Edge." *Business Week Online*, 22 September 2005.

———. "Inside the Growing Empire of America's Lifestyle Queen: Martha Inc." *Business Week*, 17 January 2000, 72.

Byrnes, Nanette, Amy Borrus, and Lorraine Woellert. "The Martha Mess Becomes a Monster." *Business Week*, 5 June 2003.

Byron, Christopher. *Martha Inc*. New York: John Wiley & Sons, 2003.

Creswell, Julie. "Will Martha Walk?" *Fortune*, 25 November 2002, 121.

Farrell, Greg. "Stewart Painted as Liar, Honest Victim." *USA Today*, 28 January 2004, 01b.

Farrell, Greg, and Theresa Howard. "Stewart Takes Steps to Reclaim 'Good Life.'" *USA Today*, 16 September 2004, 01b.

Gimbel, Barney, and Keith Naughton. "A Diva in Distress." *Newsweek*, 16 February 2004, 36.

Gordon, Lois, and Alan Gordon. *American Chronicle*. New Haven, Conn.: Yale University Press, 1999.

Hempel, Jessi. "The Martha Trial: With Pals Like This. . ." *Business Week Online*, 20 February 2004.

Holt, Douglas B. *How Brands Become Icons*. Boston: Harvard Business School Press, 2004.

Ignatias, Adi. "The People Who Influence Our Lives." *Time*, 18 April 2005, 46–49.

Khan, Kim. "TV Flop Takes Toll on Martha's Stock." *CNBC Market Dispatches*, 27 October 2005.

Landon, Thomas. "Stewart Deal Resolves Stock Case." *The New York Times*, 8 August 2006, C1.

Leavitt, Sarah A. *From Catherine Beecher to Martha Stewart*. Chapel Hill: University of North Carolina Press, 2002.

Madore, James T. "This 'Halfway House' Goes All the Way." *Charleston Daily Mail*, 1 March 2005.

"Martha Stewart Living Omnimedia, Inc. Announces First Quarter 2005 Results." *PR Newswire*, 26 April 2005.

"Martha Stewart Shares Her Recipe for Business Success." *The Associated Press*, 11 October 2005.

McMurdy, Deidre. "A Brand Called Martha." *Maclean's*, 4 December 2000, 49.

Medina, Jennifer, and Abigail Sullivan Moore. "Martha's Privacy Seems to be Everyone's Business." *The New York Times*, 13 March 2005, 14.

Naughton, Keith, and Barney Gimbel. "I Will Be Back." *Newsweek*, 26 July 2004, 40–41.

Naughton, Keith, Johnnie L. Roberts, Karl Gude, and Lisa Bergtraum. "Martha Breaks Out." *Newsweek*, 7 March 2005, 36–44.

Oppenheimer, Jerry. *Martha Stewart Just Desserts*. Boca Raton: AMI Books, 2003.

Orecklin, Michele. "10 Questions for Martha Stewart." *Time*, 19 September 2005, 8.

Orecklin, Michele, and Simon Crittle. "Oh, My God, Get Martha on the Phone." *Time*, 16 February 2004, 48.

Rielly, Edward J. *The 1960's: American Popular Culture Through History*. Westport, Conn.: Greenwood Press, 2003.

Schrage, Michael. "Martha Stewart." *Adweek*, 14 February 2000, 18.

Sell, Shawn. "Martha Is Looking Up." *USA Today*, 2 September 2003, 01d.

Sellers, Patricia. "Remodeling Martha." *Fortune*, 31 October 2005.

Shapiro, Laura. "The Art of Showing Off." *Newsweek*, 1 December 1986, 66.

Sherrow, Victoria. *A to Z American Women Business Leaders & Entrepreneurs*. New York: Facts on File, 2002.

Slater, Robert. *Martha on Trial, in Jail, and on a Comeback*. Upper Saddle River, N.J.: Pearson Education, 2006.

Stewart, Martha. *Entertaining*. New York: Clarkson Potter, 1982.

———. *Good Things for Organizing*. New York: Martha Stewart Living Omnimedia, 2001.

———. *Martha Stewart's Baking Handbook*. New York: Clarkson Potter, 2005.

———. *Martha Stewart's Gardening*. New York: Clarkson Potter, 1991.

———. *Martha Stewart's Pies & Tarts*. New York: Clarkson Potter, 1985.

———. *Martha Stewart's Quick Cook*. New York: Clarkson Potter, 1983.

———. *Martha Stewart's Weddings*. New York: Clarkson Potter, 1987, 1999.

———. *The Martha Rules*. New York: Martha Stewart Living Omnimedia, 2005.

Thottam, Jyoti, and Michael Weisskopf. "Why They're Picking on Martha," *Time*, 16 June 2003, 44.

Trump, Donald. "Martha Stewart." *Time*, 18 April 2005, 72.

"You Can't Keep a Good Diva Down: 'I Mean This Is My Life.'" *Financial Times Ltd.*, 30 August 2005.

WEB SITES

http://www.marthastewart.com/
Martha Stewart Everyday at Kmart
http://www.kmart.com/catalog/brand.jsp?categoryId = 913
http://www.savemartha.com/
http://www.kbhome.com/martha/
www.sirius.com/martha
www.nbc.com/The_Apprentice:_Martha_Stewart/
http://blogs1.marthastewart.com/

INDEX

About the Author

JOANN F. PRICE is a writing coach and instructor at Metropolitan State College of Denver.